The
First Jedi

Published by David James Publishing 2013

First David James Publishing edition 2013
www.davidjamespublishing.com

Cover Design: Jacqueline Stokes

A CIP catalogue record for this book is available from the British Library
ISBN: 978-0-9575610-1-4

About the Author

Allen was born and raised in the city of the oak grove, L'derry, or to use its proper name, Legenderry, in Northern Ireland. His family knew Allen was destined for space adventures when his birth coincided with the flyby of comet Kohoutek in 1974.

Allen spent about a decade studying philosophy, religion and education at the Queen's University, Belfast, where he improbably gained many new letters before and after his name. A carnivorous reader, Allen devours whatever graphic novels, self-help literature and textbooks scuttle across his path. He founded a business book club in Belfast called BookCamp, and enjoys writing reviews on Amazon.

Along with his wife and business partner Dawn, Allen runs Sensei, a training, coaching and writing consultancy based in Belfast, Northern Ireland. He has taught in the Schools of Education and Management at Queen's University. Now he works with SMEs, schools, international corporations and government bodies to help solve their learning needs in a radical, applied and playful way.

Allen's business website and blog is www.sensei-winbeforehand.co.uk. On Twitter he is @thesensei. His personal website is www.allenbaird.co.uk.

To my father, Robert Alexander Baird,
who taught me a great truth:
amor librorum non sine virtute est.

The
First Jedi

How the Galaxy's First University
Jedi Course was Destroyed by Dark Forces

by

Allen Baird

DAVID
JAMES
PUBLISHING

Contents

A Note to the Reader

This is a Jedi novel that is not a Jedi novel. I'd tell you that it's not part of the official *Star Wars* franchise but you already know it. George Lucas does not know it exists and probably never will. He and Disney have better things to do. Or so I've told my lawyers.

I like to think of it as an *indie novel*. So if you're after a book that deals with any of the film characters then abandon hope before entering. It does not and I don't want it to. There are enough passengers on that Lambda-class shuttle already thank you.

Another distinguishing feature of this novel non-novel is that I've based most of it on true events. From one perspective, it reads like a first-person *autobiography* for most of the time. Where possible, I've tried to provide proofs of what really went down in the form of links to secondary sources. You'll have to put on your thinking caps to wangle out the fictional elements should you want to. But they're not hard to figure with the Force of deduction, once you get a grasp of the two main protagonists.

Third, to put you completely off, it's more like a *training manual* than a novel in ways. In fact, some parts of it are explicitly so. The middle chapters contain an outline of the content of my university course on Jedi skills, and information on other related workshops are included too. And I've scattered various names and theories throughout the novel as clues for further study should you be so inclined.

All this makes it a hybrid of a book, I know, but that's exactly the sort of creature I find the most interesting. My favourite novels, films and music all take this both-and format, so why not my own book too? I've toyed with a name for the genre I'm aiming for with *The First Jedi* and the best I can come up with is *personal development fiction* (or PDF just to complicate matters). I'm a fan of self-help literature and always wondered what it would look like if blended with a fiction element to flesh it out and make it live. This is my first attempt to realise my vision.

Will it be my last? Partly this depends on how well it sells and what your response tells me. I've imagined *The First Jedi* as the first part in a trilogy. Market rather than mystical forces will probably decide the fate of that plan. If there is a second novel, it will most definitely focus on the dark side of shit.

So for now I'll leave you with the words of what that great Irish Jedi Dave Allen used to tell his many apprentices after a heavy session of training: *sit vis vobiscum, whatever your 'vis' might be.*

Chapter 1

Vader on the Rocks

Interior of house in Northern Ireland.
Exact place and time unspecified.
A thirty-something male named Mark sits on a floor of a room that
is empty apart from beer cans and books.

I've got a solitary poster taped to the wall of my living room, eye height, perpendicular to a dogged vomit stain on a rug. It depicts Darth Vader on a beach with the tide licking around his feet. In one hand, he holds a water filter jug, in the other an empty plastic bottle. He's trying to pour what looks like sea water from the jug into the bottle but it's spilling everywhere.

Below the scene, the caption reads, 'SENSE – This picture makes none'.

That phrase succeeds in gathering the threads of my life into a wearable cape. Consider it my family crest and motto, my personal mission statement. I once got a friend to translate it into Latin for me but I've long since lost the cigarette packet she used as a scroll.

I worshipped Darth Vader as a kid until I found out that you weren't supposed to. He was the bad guy. I was big and gangly too so I felt I had more in common with him than that blond bumpkin Luke Skywalker. I was Forced – geddit? – to change allegiance by some persuasive mini-Jedi bullies in the school playground. After that, I never respected anything again and it's all been downhill from that star-point onwards. I even stopped growing, more-or-less. But I'm getting ahead of myself.

Hello, my name is Mark and I'm an alcoholic. That's my usual line. It sounds plausible once you catch a scan at me. I look like a Mark and I wear the mask of an Irish style poteen-dependant, complete with twinkly eyes and a sly smile that could imply anything or nothing with equal ease. The only problem with this preamble is that I'm probably lying about the alcoholic thing.

It's true that I could gladly endure some de-pickling of the old liver right now, or mind, assuming they are different organs. I could even, if you asked, mouth all the right words, reproduce the twelve stages on cue. I could stay off booze steadily for fifty million years or the whole duration of a Formula One final, whichever arrives first. But after the time trial was over, the booze would be gone but I would remain.

I remember reading where Anthony Hopkins said his drunken exploits were an amazing and powerful experience. I memorized those lines. They make me laugh when I'm up to my ears in puke and all I can sense is the damp on my jeans thanks to any number of liquid possibilities.

A powerful experience.

You've heard it a hundred times before but I *could* give up whenever I want. I've been here before, you see. They may be

16

different rollercoasters but all the same common carriage, namely, me. Name me something, anything, and I'll tell you I've swilled it dry. Drink is only the latest on a long list of rocket-propelled crutches.

At primary school I spent my waking time on computer games, role-playing and cigarettes. With high school came weed and poker. University is a blur of techno-punk and affiliated substances. With the first flush of pay, I turned my attention to extreme sports and foreign ladies-of-the-night. Then, I remembered that I'd forgotten the devil's buttermilk and – in order to bring out my feminine side – online virtual worlds.

I'm thinking maybe politics next. Or mints, like Charlie Parker.

You can get addicted to anything. I know a guy who knows a guy who got addicted to bottled water. The story I heard was that he was a complete fitness bore, read all those men's health magazines and measured his food for fat with a ruler. It all left him so he couldn't last twenty minutes without a swig of pure liquid hydrogen and oxygen, packaged up in plastic for his personal facilitation. I reckon it serves him right. Anyone dumb or moneyed enough to buy water is half way to la-la land anyway.

I don't get addicted. I get hopeful, if you can distinguish between the two. I imagine that I've found my meaning of life each time, in every activity; a way to fill up the lack of feeling alive. Yes, that's the goal. But no, I haven't - only a way to spend money, time and myself.

The money has deserted me along with a respectable *curriculum vitae*. This time is a median in my life, midway towards threescore years and ten.

And myself?

Ah, there's the rattle of my post dropping in, today's big event. Just wait while I give it a look-see, will you. Go make yourself a cup of cold water.

Yeah, so, you wouldn't think from the cut of this carpet that I'm a qualified teacher, would you? What else can you achieve career-wise with a degree in Social Anthropology? I should have 'done law' but I went to a local solicitor for work experience and he scared the y-fronts off me. Your modern solicitor, according to him, is essentially an accountant with more prestige and less pay cheque. The guy did all but plead with me, if I had a shred of humanity in me, to do something else, anything else, anything worthwhile. Something I loved.

Foolish me, I listened, and now I'm landed with a useless Arts degree, while he retired early to Spain. *Olé!*

History was my favorite subject at high school, in the sense that it didn't make me yearn to puncture my eardrum with a compass prick. It was the teacher's fault. First off, he looked hard, with tats and a shaved head. Second, he made comments like, "Stuff the curriculum, I'll teach what I want." This appears *über* cool when you're fourteen. Third, he told stories.

In other classes, we tried to distract the teachers from their subjects with what they did last weekend, not that we cared about the social life of a fat, floral-dressed *petit-bourgeois*, pardon my French. It was a distraction from death-by-stupor. But we begged him for more, the whole *Dead Poets Society* deal.

I thought I could do the same *blah blah blah*.

And for this sin of presumption, I'm now doomed to stalk around job centers in this city and seek out strange new forms of work into which a former teacher could sink his dignity. Mostly, that involves marking exams papers, helping out at youth clubs and prostituting my skills in other degrading ways. My last trickle of tutoring work dried up when parents drove up and took a look at my new office, or should I say, council flat. Fair enough, child protection and all that. Now I teach hostel residents to write CVs and spell their names, which is an art akin to lightening a fire by rubbing sand grains together. I'll soon be joining them.

I need…something…to happen.

Excuse me while I peruse my mail.

A Visa card bill, electric bill (second warning), Kleeneze bumph and a charity collection plastic bag. The primordial excitement of it all, I'm set to swoon.

Ah! What's this? A brochure from our local university flogging second-rate courses for third-rate minds. Looks like my kind of thing then, he said knowingly. As J K Rowling would write it.

See, I'm talking to myself now, in the third person. I need that service Charlotte Church sung about, only for a Crazy Guy. You're driving *me* to insanit*ee*, which apparently involves the writing of puerile lyrics and shouting "eff off" a lot, so I'm half way there already.

The brochure has my neighbour's name on it but my address; a typical administrative cock-up for our grandest seat of learning. Meant for them, sent to me. So it's predestined to be mine, my precious. I'll rip open the plastic cover that clings to the brochure. I'll take a flick through it for fun. If it doesn't work out, I've gained a free coffee mat for my pains.

Let's scan the titles.

19

Conspiracy Theories and Popular Culture. Ireland in the Celtic Iron Age. The Battle for Palestine. Literature and the Occult. Faithful old *Guitar for Beginners.*

All the usual suspects.

Women and Science.

Well done to all two of them.

Wine Appreciation.

Basic First Aid.

Probably in that order.

Now we come to my favourite part, pop psychology, or as they call it here, 'Wellbeing and Personal Development Skills.' Pur-leese.

What do you call self-help you get from someone else? Help.

Careers Management in Changing Times.

Tell me about it, or not.

Interview Skills for Job Applicants.

Oh I can feel the fun brewing, can you?

Then I come to a page and blink. I read two titles. For the first time, my eyes move towards the little course description below.

Men from Mars: How to Survive in a Strange World. *"Many courses explore women's issues. This unique course is designed for men. In it, we will investigate the 'men's movements' and what it means to be male in the 21st Century. What is masculinity? Is it connected to adventure-seeking and risk-taking? Can it cope with anger and stress? What about male confidence and self-image? Are you a man or a mouse?"*

I always liked science fiction, emphasis on the fiction.

Power-plays: How to Take Control in Life. *"Do you want to get to the top and stay there? Do you want people to like and admire you? Do you want to be able to take control of any situation, or win at any game? Do you want to avoid trickery or manipulation by others? This course will unfold the tactical and psychological secrets of getting what you want."*

Gordon Gekko is alive and well in Belfast, I deduce.

Both 1-day courses, both by the same guy. Allen Baird BA, PhD.

You have got to be yanking my chain here, Al. OK, top marks for the catchy titles, complete with 'how to' hooks. And fair enough too for thinking of something different from the usual embroidery and conversational Kazakhstani. But really. You're overdosing me on 80s cheese, dude. Belfast isn't southern California. You're not Tony Robbins. Get over it. This is the country where a man who wears a waistcoat gets gaped at in the street. And a guy that visits the hairdressers for a styles cut is classified as a flaming homosexual.

I quickly flick through the section to see if Al 'Give-Me-All-Your-Money-And-I-Can-Heal-Your-Pain' Baird has any other courses for horses…or is that courses for sheep. Yes, two more, both towards the mundane side of the Force.

Hyperchoice: Decision-Making in a World of Alternatives. Yeah, it must be tough deciding what sector of the victim brigade you're going to target this time, Al

I Think Therefore I Am: Brain Skills for Doers. Brain will be provided, right? All courses are £23. No concessions. No refunds. No thanks.

Two hours later I sign up for both; the *Mars* one and the

Power, one that is.

I could tell you that I'm doing it to score or that I'm scavenging new job options. If you pushed me more I'd confess, yeah, all right, I'm curious too, it's no crime unless you're a cat. That isn't the ultimate reason though.

The end of all flesh has come before me.

Mine anyway.

Whoa, deep, I know but hear me out. I heard a priest recite it once when reading a lesson and the line stayed with me since, goose bumps guaranteed. I can't do this wasted oblivion tango anymore. I need a new mind-trick, a real-life one. It's the end of my elaborate plans and everything that stands.

The End. Thank you Jim. You knew, yes sir, you knew.

So now I'm sitting here with the brochure in one hand and an unopened can of extra strength brew in the other. I just sit here for a while, balanced between the two. Finally, I decide and pour the booze down the toilet. Right after drinking it.

See, it's not hard to give up alcohol, I can do it anytime. The trick is finding another addiction to replace it first.

It's a veritable voyage of discovery, every time. Like they say in shit novels. A powerful experience in y-fronts.

A y-wing fighter in heat.

Why?

Chapter 2

All Men Dream

A bathroom outside Belfast, Northern Ireland; in a house, obviously.
Monday 31 March 2008, 8:36 am.
Allen is in the shower.

As the water falls down to sweep the night sweat from my flesh, I feel like a man reborn. But don't take the simile too seriously, I'm prone to exaggeration.

I've opened the window but locked the door. The mist can only escape one way, out into the youngish, awaiting air. No one will enter here now.

I am alone. I smile, that is, my facial muscles relax from their assumed position of *faux* fierceness.

An Irish comedian once made the comment that males think of strange worlds for the most part. That's why we freeze when a woman asks us what we're thinking. The truth would unsettle them or embarrass us or both. So we make up something mundane instead, food or football, or deny all thinking whatever. The comedian said he dreamed of life as a spy, complete with codenames and lines of fire. For me, this morning, the question was this.

So if I had to start up a Jedi Academy for young people, how would I do it?

The first thought comes into my head. Since I'm Irish, it is of what I cannot do. I've studied a little Wing Chung kung-fu, less Krav Maga. I could teach a kid how to stand up for himself in the playground. I've shown my wife how to punch upwards with the palm of the hand and stick her thumbs in some deviant's eyes. But this is a long way from instructor status. Plus, I've no sword skills at all, none, never mind *Nunchuka* skills. So I'd need a teacher who could do all that stuff.

I imagine some generic oriental guy, maybe a little smaller than me in height. He's got that calm, inscrutable look. Maybe he's from a Shaolin background. That would be an awesome fit. Or maybe, if he's Japanese, some Aikido and Kendo. Aikido, I remember, is based on principles of defence and protection, all of which sounds seriously Jedi.

It would be a bonus if he could lead some Zen-type meditation too. I've only done beginners classes myself but my force was disturbed half way through by the sound of my own snoring.

What other skills would a Jedi require? I think of flying, or rather, piloting. Luke Skywalker distinguished himself first of all as a pilot, as did his dark father. I learned to drive late, and found

24

that it increased my coordination and confidence. There are good skills in flying and driving, life skills. Only I cannot fly...

The steam fills my lungs. A concentration of liquid heat bombards the back of my neck and flows down to the base of my spine.

This time, and with equal fancy, I picture an Eastern European chap. He's a former stunt driver or racer, I'm not too bothered which. He's bigger than me, well built, bald shaved with stubble and a few scars. He's also a pilot. Maybe ex-military, but again, mere details. Yes, I'll make him a communist too, to complete the mix. No-one can say that all the belief systems aren't represented here.

I imagine the three of us. We're quite a team, quite a team, yes. Different skills, different perspectives. The beginnings of a syllabus. Like the Scouts, only with sabres. Pure class.

I imagine myself at the opening day, explaining to the parents what it's all about, what we're intending to teach their kids. No, I assure them, there is no religious element in it; the focus is on life skills. We three hold to different faiths. There is no agenda, no indoctrination. Just learning disguised as fun, and play with a serious message. Yes, I explain, all instructors have completed child protection and first aid training. We are all insured. We are locked and loaded, good to go.

I introduce the other two instructors and describe their credentials. This is Master Bruce Lee and he is the Lightsabre Instructor. This is Master Uri Gagarin and he is the Pilot Instructor. Each gives a demonstration. Parents and kids are in awe.

Then someone asks the question: "What do you instruct?"

Cue awkward silence in brain.

That is a deep question, the sort that requires pause and a layer of Pears soap. The soap obliges. Good soap, good soap, good soap.

(I'm stalling for time to let some random thought come to rescue me. The dream is virtuous and I'd like it to last a little longer, please. Facts are secondary.)

I make an inventory of my own skill set, or at least professional endowments. I'm a teacher of sorts. Not children, adults, mostly in the workplace. Which is strange considering this dream of the day is about teaching kids to be Jedi. Anyway, I train their parents in the kind of abilities they should have learned at school but didn't because instead it seemed better to inform their minds with declensions and long division. I mean skills like how to communicate, how to control their emotions, how to concentrate, how to build up confidence. It has to begin with a 'c' or I can't teach it. Creativity. Conflict Resolution. Comedy, that's another one.

The Power of Humour: How to Be Funny.

Thank Borat for that.

I ask myself what any of this has to do with being a Jedi. A few ideas bubble up; fragments, words, broad themes, little more, but enough to trigger off a twinge of adrenaline around the back of my thighs. This bodily point is where I feel fear, too, a physical fear of heights. If I look over a cliff or tall building, even a banister, even on TV, I feel an immediate reaction just there. It's an electric pulse of liquid weakness that starts at the back of my knees and squirts up the thigh areas.

I can perceive it, I can experience myself experiencing it, but I cannot eliminate it. Yet.

26

I teach managers and company directors how to influence others. They're already better at it than me. *Do this or you're fired.* You can't beat that, short of pulling out a gun and going "bang".

I persuade them to persuade by gentler means. I tell them how to stand, to use silence and stillness as allies. I give them phrases to recite and words that strike with power in the human brain. I show them how to connect by listening and questioning; only I call these techniques by special names, the jargon of psychologists, so they get their money's worth. I make them storytellers.

Is this not some sort of Jedi mind trick? That's what it's sort of about, isn't it? OK, I've almost convinced myself. Which is sort of a mind trick, too. Then, negative emotions, fear and anger. That's the dark side. I warn them against that, I teach them emotional management and self-control.

Well, self-control sounds a little prudish, a little Victorian. I mean, I teach them Anger Management. And Confidence, which is the opposite of fear. They are all noble, healthy skills for young people to learn, yes, but does it have much to do with *Star Wars*? I want to try it out.

Then I have an idea, *the* idea, really. The Idea That Starts Stuff Off. *That* kind of idea.

It's so delicious, so ridiculous that I mentally pause, hold it in a suspended carbonite freeze and reach for the shampoo. As I do so I remember that 'shampoo' is a Hindi word but I can't recall what it means. Who cares? The use we put the word to, that's what matters. That's what matters.

Meaning is use.

Just like 'Jedi.'

I teach weekend courses at a local university. They are non-academic, part of a community outreach initiative, the *Open Learning Programme*. Pay covers the costs but for me it's worth more than money. The people there want to learn. No boss has forced them. No qualification calls out to them. They spend their hard-earned Saturdays with me to develop, to grow, to transform into something that they weren't before but could be now.

It is difficult for me to imagine anything greater in life than this, and I have a fair amount of imagination to spare, as you can see.

I allow myself some fun in designing and naming these courses. The one on comedy is a case in point. Leave the boring titles for business, not because business is boring but because businessmen are often full of an unnamed fear of play. For them, the opposite of play is work; for me, it's despair.

So instead of Diversity Training I do a workshop on ***What Men Want: How to Manage the Men in Your Life***. Interpersonal Communication becomes ***Body To Body: How to Communicate Without Words***.

You get the message.

Dare I? The brain says no. But the instincts? They, like the sex, are on fire!

I finish my shower and step out into a larger world. I make for my laptop. I believe that I have a course proposal to write. They can only say *no*. They probably will say *no*.

I type the proposal oblivious to the wet footprints that track my path from the study back to the bathroom.

I begin to act out my dangerous dream with open eyes.

28

Chapter 3

Lightsabers Not Provided

Allen Baird's home office.
Same Monday morning, 8:51 am.

I download the requisite form from the university website, print it out, and take hold of my favourite pen. My brother gave me a silver pen on his wedding day for standing in as best man. It feels smooth and swish when the point meets the page. This sounds silly, I know, but when you're used to the life of *Bic* you can only appreciate more when quality is in your hand.

As with most forms, ninety-seven per cent of this one is an expedition into the land of the Sumatran Rat-Monkey. I leave it for my friend Ron to fill in, first name Later.

He does a lot of work for me when it comes to this sort of lark. Like everybody's favourite manager, I determine to keep the most salacious lump of work for myself. So I scroll down and put the nib on the nub. After a few attempts I come up with this:

COURSE PROPOSAL

Course Title:

Please supply a short title that we can use in our brochure:

Feel the Force: How to Train in the Jedi Way

Course Description:

Please supply a description (maximum 60 words) for inclusion in our brochure. Open Learning reserves the right to edit course descriptions:

Jedi mightn't be your religion, but you're still a fan. Learn the real-life psychological techniques behind Jedi mind-tricks – mindfulness, instinct, serenity, empathy, influence, flow. Examine the larger philosophical issues behind the Star Wars universe – balance, destiny, dualism, fatherhood, fascism and bureaucracy. Discover the academic mythologist who inspired George Lucas' story. Battle your dark-side fear and aggression. Begin your own hero-quest. Light-sabres not provided!

Learning Outcomes:

Advice on describing your course in terms of its learning outcomes is provided in the Guidance Notes. Please specify a minimum of two and a maximum of four learning outcomes:

Having successfully completed this course, students will be able to:

1. *Employ a number of psychological tools to increase their personal effectiveness and well-being*
2. *Appreciate the complex philosophical and symbolic themes*

residing within science-fiction mythos

3. *Understand the basics of the academic theories of Joseph Campbell*

It looks all right to me, in an "I dare you to, oh go on then!" kind of way. I can't imagine how the academics at the university will take to it. Well, that's a lie, I can, but it's not pretty. That's why I threw in all that argot about "complex philosophical and symbolic themes". Academics love that sort of lingo. It's my feeble attempt to flirt with them, to woo them into doing a naughty deed that they know isn't right but can be justified if you don't think about it too hard. Like supporting Chelsea in football.

I post it off to Open Learning headquarters and forget all about it and prepare nothing. I do read a few books by Joseph Campbell, if that counts. I find them hard graft because he writes in way that my brain doesn't appreciate. This is discouraging. I'm usually superior when it comes to reading books; they are my 'thing.'

(Personality defining question number 4: *Are you a bookworm or a computer nerd?* Bookworm and proud of it.)

Joseph Campbell was an academic mythologist who was one of George Lucas' influences when writing *Star Wars*. Campbell's writing style sweeps broadly and digs deep.

There is little in the way of definitions, even less technical jargon. He uses literature, poems, oral rites, cave paintings. For someone used to the precision of linguistic philosophy and the third-person, passive-voiced caution of journal psychology, his style is like receiving an overdose of new horizons. You have to see the whole before the parts make sense.

But, like the little Irish monks who invented whiskey, I persevere.

Chapter 4

Lenin Versus Regan

Allen's bed.
Tuesday 1 April 2008, 2:03 am.

Oh *merde*, what have I done? Everyone's going to think I'm a loony, that's for damn sure. *Teaching a Jedi course? At a university? With your reputation? What were you thinking of?*

I can foresee it now. They'll all find out, one by one: my colleagues, my buddies, my parents and brother, the whole wide world. So it's uncomfortable silences and behind-the-back-smirks from here to Christmas for me then.

Using a unique visualiation technique I've created called 'The Gollum Effect' – you remember Gollum, or Sméagol, that loincloth-draped skeleton out of *The Lord of the Rings* who talks to himself – I, well, talk to myself. It's really a conversation between the two halves of my brain, the resourceful right and the logical left.

We'll call them Kirk and Spock respectively for the sheer *Gre'Thor* of it.

Spock: "It is not logical to teach a course on what is essentially an instance of juvenile entertainment fiction as if it were more."

Kirk: "What, like us you mean?"

Spock: "I will take your attempt to argue against me rather than my point as a signal of defeat."

Kirk: "I'm only giving you an example of how fiction can affect reality and back again. Haven't you heard of *The Science of Star Trek*?"

Spock: "Granted, science does require the input of imagination to break past outmoded ways of thinking. Einstein's thought experiments involving sitting on a beam of sunlight are a case in point. However, in order to become valid science, all such speculations, all conjecture, must be open to testing and refutation, as when Einstein accurately predicted the procession of Mercury's orbit and the deflection of light by the Sun."

Kirk: "So you admit the place of imagination in starting out new voyages of discovery. Good. We'll make a human of you yet!"

Spock: "I hardly think…"

Kirk: "Exactly, Spock. You mistake a part of thinking for the whole."

Spock: "I distinguish fact from fantasy."

Kirk: "So you don't believe in the fact of atoms then."

Spock: "I fail to see…"

Kirk: "Right again! The first thinkers who wrote about atoms didn't then have any scientific basis for it. Science as we

34

know it wasn't even born. Yet their fantasies turned out to be true. In fact, their fantasies caused our discovery of atoms. We wouldn't have thought about them, searched for them, expected them, otherwise."

Spock: "Coincidence is not causality. They believed in dragons too. But we found none."

Kirk: "Haven't you heard of dinosaurs?"

Spock: "We have the bones of dinosaurs. They are not primitive fiction. They are now scientific fact."

Kirk: "I'm sure they're happy with the promotion. But they started off life as children's fairy tales. That's why they still excite the imagination, which in turn drives more scientific enquiry. Child-like enthusiasm and curiosity are the heartbeat of science. How many archeologists do you think started their careers as kids standing in a museum, looking with awe at the bones of some giant diplodocus?"

Spock: "But they did not end their careers there. They grew up. They replaced stories with science. To call them back to the stories would be ask them to renege on their adulthood. Stories are for children. Science is for adults. Wisdom is learning to distinguish between the two."

Kirk: "What if we're not yet adults when it comes to what Allen wants to teach? What if we're still in the child stage of development?"

Spock: "You means in terms of personal development, self-actualisation, realising our potential?"

Kirk: "I mean figuring out the full extent of what it means to be human. Something you should understand."

Spock: "Dr Baird is completely aware that *Star Wars* and

the Jedi are not fact. Indeed, I am confident that he would argue this point against detractors if it came to it."

Kirk: "The early pioneers of atoms and dragons didn't know that their theories we're going to be proved true in a couple of thousand years. They were just thinking about it, seeing what would happen, hoping for future fruit. Why is this any different?"

Spock: (pause) "Are you suggesting that Dr Baird's course might set off a chain of events that could in a few thousand years lead to the founding of a real Jedi or Jedi-like grouping?"

Kirk: "Can you prove now that it won't?"

Spock: "Of course not. Such a hypothesis could only be falsified over time, that is, if it did not in fact lead to what you suggest."

Kirk: "It's like throwing a stone into the pond and waiting to see where the ripples with take you."

Spock: "Over-used similes such as that are of limited value as evidence. But to extend it for the sake of argument, it is more likely that people in this case will look at the stone-thrower and reflect that throwing stones into ponds is an activity most usually associated with a wastrel rather than a specialised andragogist."

Kirk: "You think Al would lose his reputation."

Spock: "Such as it is, yes. Jedi training courses are the staple of unemployed computer enthusiasts and those who refuse to mature. Dr Baird trains businesspeople, professionals, corporations and the like. To them, the idea of training lifelong learners to be Jedi is more than faintly ridiculous. It is incomprehensible. It reeks of amateurism, eccentricity, or both."

Kirk: "You misunderstand and underestimate the modern workplace. There's a thirst for innovation and creativity there like never before. Corporate storytelling. The play ethic. These are all signs of a right brain revolution, Spock. Your days are numbered, my friend."

Spock: "If I may inject some facts, Jim. Profit over loss. Efficiency drives. Long hours, hard work and attention to detail. This is the reality of workplace success. Everything else is fiction and therefore unfounded in this context."

Kirk: "That's not work your describing, its purgatory!"

Spock: "Purgatory is an outdated, illogical concept."

Kirk: "Couldn't have said it better."

Spock: "Neither could you *do* better."

Kirk: "Prove it!"

Spock: "I can't. Only Dr Baird and time can."

Kirk: "Then let's loose him and let him go."

Spock: "Meaning what precisely?"

Kirk: "Meaning an experiment. The only way to see if he's done the right thing is to watch what happens."

Spock: "By then it might be too late."

Kirk: "The quest for knowledge is risky."

Spock: "True. But it must also be a measured risk."

Kirk: "All right. Let the first measurement be made by his superiors. If they accept it, there must be some merit."

Spock: "Some, yes."

Kirk: "And as for what happens then, well, we'll take it from there."

Spock: "I can see you've through this through with your usual pedantry."

Kirk: "Sometimes you've got just got to explore; to boldly go, and all that."

Spock: "Which essentially means that whatever happens, happens."

Kirk: "You can't beat the logic of that now can you, old friend?"

Spock: "Indeed."

Indeed.

I remember reading somewhere that the greatest question a human being can ask himself is, *What if?*

What if you taught a Jedi course at your local university and everyone thought you were ridiculous?

What if you used *Star Wars* to teach kids and adults important skills that they should have learned at school but didn't because they were too busy being slowly bored to death?

What if you found a way to make learning fun?

What if you could make people flourish by making them the fantastical Jedi?

What if man tried to go to the moon?

What if?

What if the university tells you to take a long jump off a short sail barge into a large sarlacc pit?

What if I start teaching and nobody knows any of my references (like the one in the last sentence)? Or too many, and I end up deal with an attack of clones who know the first name of the first guy who played Bobba Fett?

What if *what if* becomes *so what*?

And by the way, it's Jeremy, but I had to look it up.

Chapter 5

Erasmus Microman

Allen's hallway, directly adjacent to letter flap.
Saturday 7 June 2008, mid-morning.

They said yes. I can't believe it.

I cannot believe it.

The letter I've just opened is from the local university. They've accepted my Jedi course proposal. It's going ahead.

If they get the numbers to sign up, that is.

That's how it works. Someone like me writes a proposal. It goes to a committee. They read over it. If they like it, it goes in the brochure. If not, it lands in the bin and you get the academic equivalent of a Dear John letter. The brochure winds its way to thousands of homes and libraries across Northern Ireland. Of those, a percentage read through it while the rest use it as a free devise on which to plant their coffee mugs. Some of them proceed to book a place on a course that appeals to them. If enough like-minded beings exist, usually enough to cover basic room expenses and tutor fees, then the course moves from dream to reality.

I haven't reached the tipping point of certainty yet but I am at least half way there. It strikes me that I had better do some work on it, just in case sort of thing.

I could do this by watching all six films for the nineteenth time. This does not appeal.

Or I could buy some of the books on *Star Wars* that are available from Amazon. After a quick check, I see that these fall into two categories.

First I see there are seemingly hundreds of *Star Wars* novels covering, I presume, events that happened before and, more particularly, after the films. I've read a few of these before and remain unimpressed. Luke Skywalker's and Han Solo's kids all need a few months in a young offenders institute or similar boot camp for spoilt rich bratz (as far as I can sense). If I read the phrase 'reach out with the Force' without explanation one more time I'll do some reaching out myself, and it shall be with *some* force, though not with *the* Force. Anyway, these books don't give me what I need.

The second type of *Star Wars* book has potentially a bit more *utilitas*. (Sorry about the Latin. I always do that when I'm analysing. It makes me feel smarter than I am.) They chew over *Star Wars* from a more thematic perspective, such as that of philosophy or religion. So you can dig up books with titles like *The Phenomenology of the Force* and *What if Jesus was a Jedi?* You can't really, I made them up, but you get the picture. These I reject too. I want something with a little more of a 'how to' flavour about it. As far as I can tell, no such book exists.

Right then, I think, with the naivety of semi-youth, *I reckon it's up to me.*

I feel some need to go *ad fonts*, back to the sources. I'm a Renaissance Man after all, and a Protestant to boot. Isn't there an ancient text to trawl through, a sacred font of Jedi knowledge?

I'm a reader, that's what I do, that's who I am. I like to feel the paper between my fingers when I skive. What could I feel up in the *Star Wars* world?

What else but the scripts?

Google: *"Star Wars scripts."*

Top of the list, ma, top of the list!

Chapter 6

The Luzhin Attack

Mark, lying on a bed.
Belfast City Hospital, Northern Ireland.
Monday 17 March 2008, after teatime.

You have to pay for the films you watch in hospital now, did you know that?

The film is the third new *Star Wars* movie, the one where Vader turns to the dark side. He acts more like another angst-ridden adolescent than a dark lord. If Obi-Wan had given him a slap he'd have been well in order.

He should have said, "Oi, Skywalker, no! Much as I respect your ability to fly through the air with the greatest of ease and defeat Count Dooku single-handedly when only in the last film we couldn't do it together. If you don't turn off the sulking, I'll tell your mommy on you. Whoops, wrong threat…"

That first course at Queen's I enrolled for, the *Men From Mars* one, was cancelled, I don't know why, maybe the Martians did not come in peace, or at all. I couldn't get to the second on account of me arranging to kill myself, which happened to get in the way. I emailed the tutor to see if the git would send me the notes. I paid for them after all. I've paid for everything.

But, fair play to him, he sent them to me. So I printed them off and now I'm lying here on my back in a hospital, ward twenty-three no doubt, reading notes about personal power. In between times, I'm glancing at my bandaged forearms and watching a film about a young man who screwed up his life because he didn't want others to die, first name Annie.

As Alanis Morissette might suggest: by feck that's fierce ironic.

Hospitals are bizarre places. In the jargon of anthropology, they're what's known as *liminal*. Whoa Nelly, you're thinking right now, look at the size of the cortex on that one, is it Mark you're called or Albert. I'll explain if you'll let me get a word in edgeways. *Liminal* denotes a place that exists between places, not one nor the other. Like a border between two countries. Northern Ireland – is it British or Irish? Like *The Twilight Zone* off the telly; somewhere where the normal rules don't apply, somewhere that's inhabited by strange, hybrid creatures with their own agendas. Which kind of takes us back to Northern Ireland, doesn't it?

A hospital is a place between health and death, between your bedroom and the funeral parlour. I've spent most of my working life in another liminal space – the classroom. There, you're between ignorance and knowledge, infancy and adulthood.

Last night, I almost ended my life in a similar place, the

43

bathroom. Finely balanced between coming and going. Should I stay or should I go, *a la* The Clash. I tried to go in a half-arsed sort of way. It's embarrassing to scratch your wrists and then become so bored waiting to die that you phone the ambulance just to make something happen. Shite, I even had the strength to lift these notes and bring them with me.

The doctor's notes are interesting. I refer to the quack who wrote the course not the one who's keeping me alive. Some of the content I can recollect from my purple hazy university days; I can still remember a little of this stuff from Sociology 101.

Power is the ability to make choices or influence outcomes. Different groups in society wield power over others due to dozens of factors. J K Galbraith's *Anatomy of Power*, power based on force, resources or persuasion; Alvin Toffler's *Powershift*, power from violence, wealth and knowledge, much the same thing; Raven and French's study on *The Bases of Social Power*. Which are – position, personality, expertise, information, reward and punishment. So there.

Thankfully, the course notes don't linger on modern power-movements like Marxism and Feminism, or the Lefties and the Lesbos as we tagged them. Yawn. Instead, they cover the tactics of power, most of which are new to me. There's good 'ol Machiavelli with his realist political theory. Then some guy called Robert Green who wrote *48 Laws of Power*.

My fascination keeps my cynicism at bay, even when I detect a drift from the academic to the populist as the notes progress. They end with a bit on Tony Robbins, a power guru (read 'sophist') and his use of powerful decisions, questions and metaphors to change one's life. Despite myself, I'm drawn to these

44

and get sucked into trying the exercises in my head.

Anyway, Dr Baird – may I call him Bairdy? – includes an affluence slash effluence of material that I'm not *au fait* with, so I don't feel too financially shafted. He delves into Psychology and Philosophy quite heavily.

I don't want to bore you or more importantly myself so I won't rhyme off any more names. Except one. Fredrick Nietzsche. Self-proclaimed antichrist. Outcast. Madman. Genius. Shaper of the modern world. Prophet of the Superman. Reducer of all to will-to-power. And all-round champion in an 'I Wouldn't Want to Be Marooned With...' contest.

I linger over this, *"All things are subject to interpretation; whichever interpretation prevails at a given time is a function of power and not truth."*

I glance at the screen. An asthmatic robot who seems in charge has captured the Trainspotting actor and his pubescent trainee. The big wheeze mocks them, and says, in traditional baddie lingo, *we've been waiting for you, that wasn't much of a rescue.* McGregor quips, *that depends on your point of view.* Apparently it does, my old haggis-munching *muchacho*, apparently it does.

Does the value of my life so far depend on a point of view? On *my* point of view if I'm powerful enough, on someone else's if not. That seems to be the way of it. You give yourself your own value or allow the market to do it for you.

From one perspective, my story is one of an amoral, self-indulgent, addicted smart-ass, whose life follows the same narrative arc as Jimmy 'The Slang' Riddle's. I've squandered my college education and my career plays like a Tarantino film without the bloodshed. Ah, not quite true, I've shed a few drops of my own blood recently, haven't I? Now here I am.

From another perspective? Can I find the power to look at the same pile of parrot-droppings that is my life and make it talk, who's-a-clever-boy-then, even make it sing?

A doctor waddles toward me across the lino, maybe she can offer clarity.

She resembled a posh Rosanne Barr, posh for Northern Ireland anyway, which means that she once rented out Mel Gibson's *Hamlet* on DVD and pouts when she has to drink tea other than Earl Grey. I drink Earl Grey but that's different. Quack, quack.

"Good morning Mr. Black!" she shouts *en route* to the curtain.

I only have two syllables in my name, Mark Black. That always disappointed me as a boy. When anyone mentioned my name, the sound was over too quickly. Mark Black. Mark Black. (Mark *Gilmartin* Black if you want my full title, on my mother's side.) Who has a surname like Black and calls their son Mark? A chartered accountant and a primary school teacher, that's who, with the combined imaginative prowess of a trip to the Giant's Causeway. Half of the letters are the same! It's not like you have to pay for extra letters. Horatio Kane. There. *That's* a name. *That's* how to do it with knobs on. Hannibal Smith. Cameron Poe. Leopold Bloom. Obadiah Stane. Nicholas Urfe. Damien Thorn.

Sebastian Shaw.

Gilmartin Black?

"Mr. Black?"

"Yes?"

"Are we alright?"

Look at me when you ask a question, bitch. Throw me that meager level of courtesy.

"I'm recovering from a botched suicide attempt so I'm in the not alright category. Are you alright?"

"So let's take a look at your details."

She lifts an ashen, plastic clipboard at the foot of my bed and rolls her eyes across it. Her fingers flick over the pages as if she has a sample of mucus – that's snot to you and me – on her thumb that she's keen to swipe off.

Probably does too.

"The wounds weren't deep," she says.

To my untrained ear, that sounds more like a lyric from a Country 'n' Western soundtrack than a medical diagnosis. To my trained ear, however, it sounds like a slight. *You're not really sick at all. You didn't top yourself properly. You just want attention, you pathetic little man. I see your kind in here every day and you make me sick.*

Now I can't really read her thoughts, I can't perform those mind-tricks. But still, my instincts cry out in unison, *what a bitch.*

"Nurse will be around shortly to take some tests," she says.

"Is he sick too?"

"Huummm. Who?"

"Shortly," I say.

"Right," she says, the up-market equivalent of *whatever.* She wobbles off, head held high, keeping dignity and humour ratios at inverse proportion. Me? I'm still in bed. Everything in the world is where it should be.

I've hardly got back to my notes when the nurse comes in.

She looks about twelve, maybe thirteen years old. Since I remember vividly what it's like to be that age I feel happy about engaging her in conversation.

"So Mark, do you mind if I take a look at your bandages?"

"Yea. I mean no, go ahead. What's the doctor's problem, then?"

She recovers well from my audacious probing, managing her best to look hard-bitten like all the others.

"Which one?"

"The one that's just away. The fat one," I say.

"I don't know. Stick your arms out there for me please. Wrists up."

I comply.

"I think her name was Yavin or something."

"Dr Yavin is a very smart person. She'll make consultant within the year."

She carefully cuts the old bandages and I keep my eyes fixed on her so I won't have to look at what I've done to my own flesh.

"Smart in some ways. She didn't major in bedside manner, I take it."

This is a daring statement for me to make out loud. Doctors of medicine are social gods in Northern Ireland and therefore unassailable in thought, words or deed, especially words. I usually keep such gems as part of my internal monologue.

"She's battled through a lot to get where she is." She glances at the TV screen. "I was going to replace these old bandages with fresh ones. But your healing powers must be strong. I'm going to leave them open and let air get at them as much as possible. Just be careful not to scrape them against anything."

"Thanks," I say. I want to ask after Dr Yavin's battle but the nurses face says *I've said too much already, please let's leave it at that. I love my job.* I'm improving my mind-reading skills – also known as giving a shit for someone, anyone else, and looking them in the face – so I let it go. But I still wonder as she walks away. What demons did the doctor face? Was she alone? Or did she wish she was? I know that I'll never know but that's alright because as Donald Rumsfeld says there are some things that we know we don't know and if he didn't know everything then I'd prefer not to either.

Because I don't know anything I go back to watching TV.

The guy who's pretending to act like the young Darth Vader is having a chat with some old bloke. He's the emperor because he does all the talking. He's telling the boy that *good is a point of view* and that *the Jedi point of view is not the only valid one.*

The Sith are only evil *from a Jedi's point of view. The Sith and the Jedi are similar in almost every way*, mostly in their *quest for greater power.* The *difference between the two* is the Sith are not afraid of their dark side, which is why they are the most powerful. The Sith think *about themselves* but the Jedi *care about others.*

Deep for a kids' show. Too deep for me now. I throw aside my notes and pick up the remote control instead, keeping the wrists facing up.

I flick over to another channel but it's showing an old, Japanese black-and-white film with lots of samurai running around and looking ponderous. I crave some light entertainment so instead I watch a documentary about obese Americans and bask in that sense of unearned superiority we all appreciate from time to time. You know, like the kind parents feel on the birth of a baby. Both are a way of achieving something but without the requirement of talent.

Next day I'm away.

Chapter 7

Master of My Universe

Blog by Allen on 31 March 2008.
By The Power of Greyskull!

Imagine you had the power to create an entire workshop on some personal development topic that interests you but that no-one else seems to cover. What would the topic be?

I had great fun recently facilitating a workshop in personal power; I gave the rather Machiavellian title of *Power-Plays: How to Take Control in Life.* We began by looking at some of the key thinkers on the subject of power, starting with Machiavelli himself and his modern incarnation, Robert Green.

After these introductions, we explored the challenges of gaining power over your mind, power over your life and power over others.

At the end of the workshop I issued a challenge to the participants. We'd been working through the different ways of influencing others (such as arguing, asserting, empathising and energising). My class gained much pleasure from trying out these techniques on each other. This culminated with them testing out their new found powers on me!

The final exercise of the day was this:
"Congratulations! You now have a significant set of persuasion weapons in your armoury. Use them to try to persuade me to design and deliver a workshop in the Autumn on a topic that really interests you but that no present course covers. Let the games begin!"

I meant this exercise in all seriousness. Ever since I've started designing and delivering public courses for Queen's University, I've tried to tackle something different each time. So far I haven't repeated any course. I'm always on the lookout for new ideas.

The class came up with three ideas:

- Body Language
- Happiness
- Flirting Techniques

Did they persuade me?

Not so long ago, I did run a 1-day workshop at QUB - *Body To Body: How to Communicate without Words*. It was the most popular course of its kind I've created so far, with well over thirty participants. I'm giving serious thought to running it again. What do you think?

Happiness is big business these days and is roughly equivalent to such popular phrases as *well-being* and *quality of life*. I've covered such themes as *optimism* and *positive thinking* in my courses on Emotional Intelligence. But the notion of focusing in on this one theme is proving hard to resist. Should I?

And as for flirting... I'm running a course called *What Men Want: How to Manage the Men in Your Life*. So - I'm no stranger to the problems of communication between the sexes; gender relations at work is a specialist topic of mine. But flirting? The closest I'll come to this hot topic is in the forthcoming workshop *Confidence Conversations: How to talk in Any Situation*. But I will say that we are planning more workshops on these sorts of themes in the near future. Watch this space!

I'd really love to hear your ideas for public course topics. What interests you? Let me know and you could have a course specially designed for you!

Chapter 8

Red Button Times

Somewhere off the King's Road, Belfast.
Tuesday, April 1, 2008.

I have to see a psychiatrist about my suicide attempt but only an NHS one so I'm not expecting a leather couch or any other middle-class type reclining device. But I do demand some talk about my childhood and my dreamscape and whether I want to marry my mother.

Instead, they hand me a sheet of photocopied paper with one of the corners crunched up and blurred grey. I'm told that this is a pre-session client interview.

I induce brain strain in my quest to imagine how the counsellor will study it and analyse it adequately in the ten minutes between now and our first pow-wow.

This is what I write down, I swear on my father's grave,

him who I apparently aspire to murder even though he did me no harm. Not that he did me any good either, but at least I broke even with him, which is as much as any son has the right to expect in this broken society.

Have you ever received therapy, counselling or any similar treatment?
Yes, in Northern Ireland we call it alcohol. That's what got me here, a little too much of the liquid remedy. Beyond that, no, unless you count the Chinese fortune cookie I opened once. It said "*A conclusion is simply the place where you got tired of thinking*", which I thought was unnecessarily profound for a Friday night in Toome.

Are you currently any form of medication?
See above.

What are your reasons for approaching this counselling service?
The fat woman doctor at the hospital sent me, you know, the one who has had her own battles but is very smart.

What are you hoping to gain from counselling?
Although it's a tortured cliché it would be nice if someone gave me a reason for not killing myself so then I wouldn't try to kill myself and have to go to hospital and eventually see you again or maybe god/the devil first because sometimes I imagine a big red button in front of me and if I press it the world would be as if I never existed and if I don't press it then things go on as they are and for most of my life my finger is hovering over the button and for some

unknown reason even in my mind I can't bring myself to press the button so it seems there is something in life I want to cling on to but I don't know what it is because technically I'd rather be annihilated or in a state of non-being as in Nirvana but the Buddhists mightn't be right so I might end up in purgatory or hell for ever and the odd the very odd time life is good but for most if it I'm unhappy or bored so in percentage terms it would make more sense not to live but I know that there is no single answer you can give me and its more likely that you'll ask me a pile of questions and expect me to come up with the answers myself but what do I know I don't even know if I believe in god or the Force or whatever it is I guess probably exists out there somewhere so instead I have to stick to what I know which is that being blitzed on drink or drugs is the closest I can safely come to being dead and then resurrected afterwards so for a brief moment it's like I've pressed that red button in a virtual sort of way even though I haven't really pressed it but I don't care really if the reason you give me to go on is real or made up so long as it does the job of adding some magic to my life yes that's what I want because the comic side of life and the tragic side of life are sort of merging into one and I'm exhausted with lurching between the two as I need something to make me feel alive rather than existing as an object among other objects if you forgive the philosophical musings because I'm not a certified genius though I've got a degree but that doesn't count anymore even if it's a Geoff Hurst and even though they wanted me to do a post-grad but I couldn't afford it so I became a teacher instead as I got funding for the qualification and what else was I to do when she left me or rather left the country for the arse end of nowhere to study that tribe who frown when they're happy or whatever it was to make her mark but not her Mark while I sneered at such pretentions as I do about everything and we argued about the point of it all and I said that it started with a big bang and would end with a big crunch both the universe and our relationship and anything in between was waiting for a bus that would never come and she said why not just end it now if that's how you feel but I said it wasn't a personal insult just a point of view and she said what about me am I not enough and I said while you're waiting at the bus stop it's better to be amused than bored and she said she was no-one's fucking plaything and if I couldn't commit I should go back to my weed and poker and waste my life away so that's what I did to prove her right with her superior overachieving father with the only respite coming when I lost myself in my books and essays and studies which were the only thing that made me excited or at least interested apart from her so why didn't I go with her and do research together I'll never know and it's too late now because she's engaged and my brain is fried and my one chance is wasted and that's about it so unless you can build me a time machine or magic up a new world for me to live in then I don't feel that I have much to gain from this counselling game at all no offence to you.

On a scale of 1 to 10 (10 being the most serious), how seriously is your condition affecting your quality of life?
Minus 42

How have you been coping with your problem until now?
By playing free, online computer games and watching YouTube all day. Sentimental gorging on HP Lovecraft and REM at intervals of about four months as a substitute for intellectual activity. The odd

venture into Eastern mysticism. And sleeping as much as possible.

Can you identify any way in which you might be contributing to the problem?
I am human. I am Mark Black. Ergo etc.

Is there anything important we should know?
As a hobby I'm thinking about training as a dark lord of the Sith. Which is nice. Why? I could do a better job than Hayden Christianson who can't act to save his life. This isn't saying much of course since Sooty would also be an improvement but it's a start.

I take a fit of the silent sniggers at this last scrawled entry and try to suppress it. Then I picture some seventy-year-old fop who's too health conscious to even smoke the obligatory Calabash telling me with a Viennese accent that repression is complex-forming and I should let out all my laughter in one cathartic, primal bellow.

Just as quickly as it appears, the image melts into a sensation of black acid, surging from somewhere between my oesophagus and my small intestine. So I saunter out for some air, leaving the badly photocopied sheet of paper lying on the seat.

I don't think anyone notices when I fail to return. At least I don't. And that's the main thing.

Chapter 9

Angry Youngish Man

Blog by Allen on 8 August 2008.

Men From Mars Waste Their Hours

Why do men show so little interest in Lifelong Learning or self-improvement? Even - or especially - when it comes to learning about themselves?

I've taught lots of courses at Queen's University Belfast in the field of Personal Development. These workshops have ranged from Memory Improvement to Body Language, from Emotional Intelligence to Influencing Skills. They were all very well attended. But at a highly conservative estimate, the ratio of females to males in each class was about 5:2. Last year I had four more scheduled: Decision Making, Thinking Skills, and Personal Power were the first three. A great number of students signed up for each one. I had about 20 per class. But the fourth one? It was on Masculinity. And the interest rate? Zero. Well, that's not exactly true. Two brave guys signed up for it, but this wasn't enough to allow the class to go ahead.

Now I know what you're thinking. 'Masculinity' sounds more like a medical procedure than a course you might be interested in attending.

Here's how I pitched it in the university brochure:

It's a one day workshop. And a snip at £23. So why no interest? Well, that's not entirely true either. A journalist showed some interest. *She* said she would love to sit in as an observer. I told her we first needed something to observe. If you want more on this theme, read my blogs *Why Are Men Such Fat, Stupid Wasters? #1 & #2*

Chapter 10

Knowledge and Defence

Interior of another flat in Belfast, Northern Ireland
Tuesday 12 August 2008, 11:45 am.

Because I booked those two courses, they've sent me another brochure, even though I haven't attended one yet. I keep saying brochure but its proper title is the *Open Learning Programe 2008-2009 Autumn*.

Ooh la la!

Out of morbid curiosity, I flick through it again and zero in on courses by Dr Allen Baird. Big surprise, he's got a few, the guy's obviously a relentless self-promoter. I'm telling you the absolute truth when I divulge what they are.

The Psychology of Happiness: How to Grow Your Happy Skills
Are you stuck with your feelings, or can you make yourself happier

in a more enduring way? What concrete attitudes and lifestyles should you adopt in order to do so? This workshop will teach you to enhance your sense of well-being through the scientific study and imitation of those skills shared by optimistic, fulfilled people. Our commonest cause of unhappiness – work – will receive special focus.

The Power of Humour: How to Be Funny

What if you were told there was a single secret to job promotion, relationship success, personal popularity, and mental well-being? What if this secret also boosted your powers of problem-solving and creativity? This secret is – the capacity for humour, or looking at life's comical side. Learn to develop this skill by analysing what humour is and how to use it for your advantage in everyday life.

The Main Thing: How to Find Meaning in Your Life

Do you sometimes feel your life lacks sense or significance? Join the club! Our search for meaning is the most basic human drive... and the most misunderstood. A lack of personal meaning leaves you without purpose – powerless, passive, and pessimistic. Learn how to give meaning to your own life by employing a range of practical techniques, from powerful questions to personal stories.

And one on *Star Wars*.

No way.

Yes way.

The courses on happiness and meaning would beyond doubt have a special significance to me after my suicide attempt.

So I carefully weigh up my present, deep-seated needs and

spend whole seconds matching these up with the course or courses that I judge would most benefit the psycho-somatic malady that afflicts me.

Then I sign up for the Jedi workshop.

Chapter 11

The Order of the Binary Sunset

Allen's home study

Monday 25 August, 2008 (Bank Holiday)

It's an enlightening experience, reading the scripts of the six *Star Wars* movies. You learn much that's not in the films.

For instance, did you know that Princess Leia is only supposed to be eighteen in *A New Hope*? Or that the stormtroopers are described as wearing "fascist, white armoured suits?" Or that Luke recites a mantra to calm himself before destroying the Death Star?

It's all there. These little hints and clues help me build up a grander picture.

I have to admit too that I'm not coming at this task with a blank slate. My head is full of material – ideas, theories, techniques, authors, mostly single words – gleaned from my experience. I'm on the prowl. I underline, italicise, increase or in some way alter anything in the scripts that I think might be useful. Then I trawl through them again to try to pick out clear, recurring themes. When I discover one, I create a document – I'm sure you want to know all this – and paste in it all the references to that theme. When I'm finished, there are fifty-four of these themed entries, from 'Adventure' to 'Wise Old Man'. Fine for me that I've nothing better to do such as cutting my front lawn; it resembles Endor out there.

I steal from YouTube. There's a wealth of resources for me to plunder here, goodies of all kinds. There are plenty of clips from the films – Luke with Ben, Luke with Yoda, Luke with Vader, all the key moments – if one is allowed to use them. Please don't sue me George, they're for education purposes only. I'm your biggest fan, and I know where you live.

I totally dig the humorous clips. There's the *Jedi gym* and the *Jedi church*. There's *The Emperor's Job* and *The Emperor's Phone Call*. I particularly recommend *How Star Wars Should Have Ended* (along with the others in this series); it was scary to realise that my own serious contemplations on *How Lord of the Rings Should Have Ended* were shared by someone else. There is a *Dead Ringers* sketch that is based on a telling truth (as is the *Man in the Box* sketch), and another one about buying a car - Jedi style. *Chad Vader Dayshift Manager* is too long, although richly comical. Elsewhere Vader pops up playing golf and serving in the Death Star canteen.

Most important for me at an emotional level – I feel we know each other well enough – was the discovery of my two favourite *Star Wars* scenes. The first is a thirty-four second pulse of cinematic genius usually called the 'Twin Setting Suns' or the

Binary Sunset scene. It lumpifies my throat every time. If I had to start up a secret Jedi organisation today, I'd call it *The Order of the Binary Sunset*. The music, Luke's sense of longing and frustration, familial chores, the uncharted horizons beyond, who hasn't been there?

Then we have the Funeral Pyre scene in which Luke lays to rest the shell of his now-reconciled father, then seeing him live on as a Force wraith.

In both clips, there is never a spoken word, but they exude a power that's palpable; as long as it doesn't become palpatine, we're safe.

Anyway, I'd love to sit and jowl but I don't have the time. You see, shortly after I obtained word that they accepted my course, the course catalogue containing it and all the others was published.

I received a copy. So did every former student.

So does the local press and media.

Then all Hoth breaks loose.

Chapter 12

Platformed News

Classified Information – FYEO

This is an email sent from Allen to a prominent Belfast journalist who had requested information prior to meeting up. Names and stylistic weaknesses have been altered for publishing purposes.

Sent – Thursday 28 Aug 2008

Hello Red Fox

Thanks for doing conducting an interview with me on this course.

I think I'll give you a little background before we talk on the phone as it might set the scene.

I'm a training consultant, so I normally provide training in management topics for businesses (Time Management, Communication Skills, Assertiveness, Emotional Intelligence, Business Ethics etc.)

However, I've come to realise that the principles that form

the basis of my business workshops would be of great use to the general public. So, about four years ago I made some workshop proposals to QUB for inclusion into their excellent Open Learning Programme. They proved a great success. Since, I've developed courses on memory improvement and learning skills, conversation and persuasion skills, and body language. This last course has proved so popular that I'm repeating it this year!

The main reason I'm running the Jedi course is that I'm trying to make life-skills exciting and accessible for those who mightn't otherwise be interested. For instance, most of those who come to my workshops tend to be older and female. However, I'm trying to broaden the target audience because I think the topics are universally applicable.

The Jedi workshop is really about providing a fresh platform from which to discuss some of the issues in personal development and our role in contemporary society.

For instance, in the *Star Wars* films, there is mention of the Jedi's ability to use to mental states of 'flow' and 'mindfulness' to achieve their aims. Most people remain unaware that these are mental states that have been the subject of serious academic, psychological research.

Also, a Jedi must battle such negative emotional states as anger and fear. And, it just so happens that we regularly encounter these in our lives. So, I'll be looking at how psychology can help us to control and even turn these feelings to our advantage.

On top of this, the *Star Wars* saga raises all sorts of questions about society and our role in it. The good guys are 'rebels' because they don't accept the evil Empire. Is it ethical to resist tyranny? How far can we take this? The Empire is portrayed as a bureaucratic, machine-dominated system that removed people's humanity. Doesn't that sound similar to our world of high-technology but low empathy?

The Jedi, by contrast, are so skilled at empathy that they can read and influence the minds of others. Of course, I can't teach these tricks, but I can teach people to how read non-verbal communication cues and wield words persuasively.

I would describe myself as a minor sci-fi fan. I did collect *Star Wars* figures as a young boy, but I've never been to a *Star Wars* convention, nor dressed up as a Jedi.

I have however watched all the films (the first three were best) but I haven't read many of the more recent saga's books. And I don't try to make out that Jedi is a religion.

Rather, I take it as a motivating and innovative way of looking at some of the issues involved in contemporary psychology and thinking.

My hope is that it will appeal to people who might otherwise think that going to a Queen's workshop would be a waste of time.

I've found that my usual classes consist of people who are interested in life-skills and who are naturally keen to learn more about themselves and their world. So my relation with the class is usually informal, with lots of interaction and discussion. That's how learning should be and that's the way I like it.

In this Jedi workshop, there will be something for sci-fi and *Star Wars* fans, films buffs, young people, and those into personal development and popular psychology. Some of the people who come to my courses are past attendees; it must mean that the quality is good.

That said, I would love to see others try it who've never been and usually wouldn't think of coming. It's a great chance to explore fresh ideas, enjoy some *craic*, meet new people and develop skills, all for the price of £23!

I hope this is of some use. I'll phone you soon.

Allen

Chapter 13

Train Them You Can

Blog by Allen on 10 September 2008

Feel the Force:
How the Train in the Jedi Way

Dismayed at the male/female breakdown of some of the personal development type workshops I run at QUB, I was thinking something along the lines of...

Young men are not so interested in personal development, what might prick their ears..? Aha! Name the course after a Star Wars theme! The ideas and techniques are similar, so that might make them think...

I got more than I bargained for, when it all kicked off on Tuesday last week.[1] Not only did the News Letter pick up on the quirky workshop title, but the Stephen Nolan Show wants to interview me at some point and the BBC NI published an online article! Then there was the 'photo-shoot' with the South and North Belfast News, the radio interviews with Radio Foyle and Citybeat...

Finally, and most surprisingly of all, the *Guardian Educational Supplement*, hot on the heels of the *Times Educational Supplement*, phoned for further information, in order to put together an article.

If you'd like to book a place on the workshop at QUB, please click for details - *Feel the Force: How to Train in the Jedi Way* (15/11/08).

Watch this space for a hooded Jedi near you!

---

[1] By this I mean the publicity kicked off, not the training event itself.

Chapter 14

Most Photographed Jedi

Feature article in Belfast Media website.

Carving out a path to creativity for all

South Belfast News

More of a space cadet than a Jedi Knight, South Belfast's most photographed guest lecturer, Dr Allen Baird, has come a long way from electrocuting the beaks off chickens, or so Alana Fearon finds out...

I was born in...

USA (up stairs in Altnagelvin)

I grew up in...

Stroke City and Ballymena.

I now live in...

Ballyclare.

I was educated at...

Clondermot High School (now defunct), Ballymena Tech ('Institute' as it is now) and Queen's University.

My earliest memory is...

My mother changing my nappy during a thunder storm.

When I was a child I wanted to be...

An explorer or a soldier of some sort.

I actually became...

A training consultant, coach and writer.

Worst job you've ever had...

Cutting the toes off chicks in a poultry hatchery and electrocuting their beaks off. I kid you not.

Best job you've ever had...

What I'm doing right now, which is making learning attractive, accessible and useful for people in work or life.

The bravest thing I've ever done...

Sitting my PhD oral exam in front of three weighty (in multiple senses) professors.

The stupidest thing I've ever done...

Run away from home as a kid and generally mess about in school.

The biggest thing I've yet to do...

Complete one of my several almost finished books and send it into a publisher.

The person/people who inspired me most is/are...

Anyone who follows their bliss and doesn't give a stuff what others say.

The most important thing in the world is...

To have a feeling that you are alive rather than merely existing.

I'm very bad at...

Doing stuff that I find boring, trivial or showy.

I'm very good at...

Listening to people and learning from my many mistakes.

I'm most proud of...

Designing and delivering courses that answer people's questions and make a difference.

My best friend would say I was...

A thinker and connoisseur of strange books.

I like to relax by...

Reading, practising martial arts, having good conversations and watching dark films.

My favourite saying/quote is...

"Be regular and orderly in your life like a bourgeois, so that you may be violent and original in your work" – *Gustave Flaubert*.

The last book I read was…

Six Thinking Hats by Edward De Bono.

My favourite book is...

Ecclesiastes (Old Testament book, better than it sounds, really).

My favourite movie is...

The Thin Red Line.

The actor that would play me in a movie of my life would be…

Edward Norton with a goatee.

The song that makes me dance is...

Break On Through (To The Other Side) by The Doors.

The song I would have played at my funeral would be…

Any Psalm.

The best place I've ever been...

Tasmania, it's like Northern Ireland only with good weather and bad roads.

The place I have to visit before I die is…

The Devil's Tower in Wyoming, USA.

The last person I talked to on the phone was...

My wife Dawn, blogging guru and business partner.

The last text message I received was from...

My brother Paul, slagging me off for being more of a space cadet than a Jedi master, which is nice.

If I was a politician I would...

Ban TV and introduce a maximum wage for footballers.

If I won the lottery I would...

Set up an academy in Northern Ireland to teach kids (and maybe some adults too) confidence, creativity and communication skills for free.

If I could describe myself in five words they would be...

Courteous, interested, thoughtful, imaginative, calm.

If I could invite five people (living or dead) to a dinner party they would be...

Marcus Aurelius, Tolstoy, Alfred the Great, Socrates and Hemingway. I can feel your excitement already.

If I could change one thing about South Belfast it would be...

More car parks or fewer cars or both.

My favourite thing about South Belfast is...

The choice of excellent cafés on the upper Lisburn Road.

Thu 11/09/2008 16:21

Hi Alana

Here it is as promised. I hope it's what you were after.

Today I've been interviewed by the Times and the Telegraph!

What next...CNN?

Allen

Chapter 15

Stand Back Clive Owen!

Blog by Allen on 12 September 2008
Jedi Workshop Goes International!

Well, kind of. I was interviewed this morning by Steve Chase of
ABC Radio, Australia.

Media coverage for the workshop has snowballed at an
unbelievable rate in the last week. Dawn mentioned some of the
radio interviews I've done in the last blog, as well as the initial
exposure with the *Newsletter* and the BBC.

This in addition to the national newspapers that were generous with
their space... at least on-line. First of all there was *The Guardian
Educational Supplement,* hotly pursued by *The Times Higher
Education Supplement.* The latest treatment was by *The Times*

Online, which is interesting because of the comments generated (not all of which are flattering). *The Daily Telegraph* is in on the act too.

Dopiest question award? "Will you be bringing a romantic element into the course, you know, Luke and Leia kind of thing?" Actually, they were brother and sister, so no, not really...

Second stupidest question award? "Will there be a dress code for the course?" Yea, smart casual should do it, hopefully smart in the head, casual in the jeans.

Most confused question? "Is this sort of course not denigrating to a great educational establishment like Queen's University?" Well, if by 'denigrating' you mean far-sighted, innovative and down-right interesting, then I suppose you have a point. Plus, it's not a degree course, you can't earn a BA in 'Jedi Studies'! Sorry to disappoint.

That's all for now, except to prove how little all this has gone to my head. If you want a laugh, go to the South Belfast News photo section to see how this Jedi made a complete *eejit* of himself, all in the name of free publicity.

There's more to tell, but this will do for now.
May the Force... whatever!

Chapter 16

That's Me in the Corner

Classified Information – FYEO

Emails One to Two – Correspondence between Allen Baird and Daniel Jones (Church of Jedi).

Emails Three to Five – Correspondence between Allen Baird and unnamed boss type person at Queen's University about issues arising from above.

For security reasons – i.e. in case somebody sues Allen's ass – only his side of the correspondence is included.

Email One

From: Allen Baird

Subject: Jedi Handbook

To: info@jedi-church.com

Date: Saturday, September 13, 2008, 11:37 AM

Greetings

My name is Allen Baird. I'm a university tutor at Queen's, Belfast (among other things) and I'm delivering a 1-day workshop in Jedi mind-skills in November this year.

I notice from your site that you give away a free 6-page Jedi handbook to those who ask. I would like a copy, please.

I've had a lot of interest in the course from around the world. I'll be putting relevant information up on our business blog in the next week or so. Although we might disagree on the status of Jediism I wish you all the best in your serious endeavors toward personal development.

Cordially

Allen

Email Two

From: Allen Baird <allen@sensei-winbeforehand.co.uk>

Subject: RE: Jedi Handbook

To: ukjedichurch@yahoo.com

Date: Monday, September 15, 2008, 4:45 PM

Hello Daniel

I think it was you I was speaking to this morning. Sorry I didn't have the opportunity to chat then.

Give me a ring anytime now and we'll talk.

Allen

Email Three

From: Allen Baird

Sent: 16 September 2008 15:33

To: XXXX
Subject: RE: jedi

Here is their 'church' website - http://www.jedi-church.com/
Here is another Jedi church website with more general info on it - http://www.jedichurch.com/
The guy is called Daniel Jones. Their church has received a lot of publicity since it opened, mostly of the 'what a freak show' variety - http://news.bbc.co.uk/1/hi/wales/7200531.stm
I think their key aim is to use the publicity created by my course to get people interested in joining their church. He told me this explicitly.
He also told me that he has been in debates in Christian churches in Wales, most of whom classified them as a cult.
He sent me some of their literature which seems to me to be a mixture of new-age beliefs and gobbledygook (see attached).
It's BBC3 that is interested in the documentary, so hardly a big deal. They boasted to me that they've been on *Trisha*!
Like I said, I am fairly strongly inclined to say no anyway, since I think any association would be damaging for the credibility of QUB and Sensei. However, I will withhold a final answer to them until I hear what you have to say.
Allen

Email Four

From: Allen Baird
Sent: 16 September 2008 16:17
To: XXXX
Subject: RE: jedi

I think what they actually wanted at the start was to come and join me in teaching the course or providing some sort of direct input! I rejected this outright. Then it moved down a notch to their being there in order to explain to interested participants what their church does and how to join it.

This smells of proselytizing to me; it goes beyond a mere discussion of religious concepts. There was even some suggestion that as the climax of the course I could debate with them whether 'Jediism' is a valid religion. I think that BBC3 is doing the piece with them anyway.

They said that the BBC might pay for their fare and course fees just to get a few shots of them with me. I do not want this association. If your main concern is censorship, then I have a few thoughts: I am quite willing to take the pressure off QUB by making this matter one of tutor discretion.

In other words, I could make the decision to refuse their offer and it could be left officially that QUB didn't say no, but I did. As I said previously, my business partner and I feel strongly that it would do damage to our professional reputation to be in any way associated with this 'church.'

But even apart from that, I don't think the BBC would cry 'censorship' on this one. The documentary will go ahead - or not - anyway. As a project, it is not dependent for its existence on our assent anyway. And their 'church' is perceived as a bit of a 'geek freak show'. That is the very reason for the documentary in the first place, I suspect. Please feel free to pass on my emails to whoever needs to see them.

Allen

Email Five

From: Allen Baird

Sent: 16 September 2008 16:38

To: XXXX

Subject: RE: jedi

No, we are not involved so far in any way. I suspect the producers of the documentary are just looking to stretch out their material a bit on the back of this new wave of interest.

I didn't intend to deal with any 'religious' aspects in my course at all.

Allen

Email Six

From: Allen Baird [allen@sensei-winbeforehand.co.uk]

Sent: 22 September 2008 09:01

To: XXXX

Subject: RE: jedi

Just to give you the latest on the Jedi church thing.

As directed, I sent them a polite but firm refusal on 16th. Since then I've heard nothing. I suspect that's the last we'll hear from them. If they do get in touch again, or if BBC3 does, I'll let you know immediately.

Allen

Chapter 17

Serious Sci-Fi

Blog by Allen on 22 September 2008.

Mind-tricks, Magic, and the Media

Interest in my Jedi 'university workshop' has, I think, climaxed. I've mentioned that I was interviewed on ABC Radio in Oz. The latest is an interview on Danish Radio Station *DR*, who were pretty into it.

So it was comforting to learn that I'm not the only ~~wacko~~ innovative, lateral-thinking teacher around. Professor Richard Wiseman has told the *British Association Science Festival* that teaching magic tricks helps pupils perform better.

They learn a cluster of social skills - like empathy, confidence, and social intelligence - that are otherwise difficult to teach.

For those of you interested to know what happening out there with the Jedi course, here's a sample of the word on the street.

The Irish News gave us a mention, as well as the global news network AHN. News websites as far away as Thailand, Australia, and Michigan State University continue to mention it.

But what do people actually think of the idea? Some of the comments made on these sites are hilarious. For interesting feedback, see Shortnews, The Register, Slashdot, and Reddit. 109 is particularly good. But when you reach the Jedi News, you know you've made the big time.

But things took a serious turn when a national business asked me if I would do a half-day speech/training session for them at their annual conference. Apparently they want someone who can make communication and inter-personal skills interesting as well as informative. Sounds like the force is strong with their training department! Let's see what happens.

Chapter 18

Remove Tongue
from Cheek. Not.

Highly Classified Information – FYEO

Below is evidence that Allen sneaked in a document to his radio interviews as an aid when answering questions.

Psychological profile: Initial analysis suggests that Baird has an inferiority complex and acute memory problems especially in the area of self-promotion and sounding like a hathog.

Tell us about the Open Learning Programme at QUB.

My workshop is part of what is called the Open Learning Programme at QUB. That means that it's open to those who don't have any formal qualifications. It's a great way for people to connect with learning again, maybe to develop a skill or explore an interest further. Or it can be a first step back into education for someone who had a bad experience at school and left without any qualifications. The only qualification is that you have to want to learn.

Why are you running a course like this?

You need to understand the differences between how you educate children and adult education. With children you can start wherever you want because they don't know much. But with adults you have to start with where they're at, what they're interested in. Otherwise, they're not interested. So, this is an attempt to get people who might not otherwise care, interested in Lifelong Learning and developing their skills.

What are you actually going to be teaching in your course?

Believe it or not, I'm actually teaching the same sort of stuff that I teach to business people and managers in my professional workshops. I teach Assertiveness, Emotional Intelligence and Communication Skills. The only difference is that I'll be using *Star Wars* to enliven attendees' imaginations and provide a framework in popular culture to connect to them. For instance I will be teaching how to use words and body language to influence people, and I'll be showing them how to control their attention and thinking as they discover now information (mindfulness).

How did this idea come to you?

Well the workshop is my attempt to solve a bit of a problem that I've discovered with some of my courses. Most of those who enrol tend to be female and 40+, which is great. But I wanted to design a course what might attract a younger audience and perhaps even out the gender divide a little.

Does this not detract from the reputation of QUB?

The Times and Guardian Educational Supplements called my course *creative* and *innovative*, so that sort of compliment enhances the reputation of QUB. But you have to take the course for what it is – it isn't a standard academic course, it's a 1-day workshop. You can't do a degree in Jedi Studies, and you shouldn't be able to. Although you can use *Star Wars* to teach other, more important things.

Isn't it all a bit childish?

Football is essentially childish – but it's also a billion dollar business that's the most important thing in the lives of many people. The fashion industry is essentially childish – but it's the same. But sometimes it's not bad to be childlike – your childhood was the time that shaped us the most, it was when we showed the most creativity and fun in discovering new things. That's what good education is all about.

How many people are signed up for the course? What sort of people do you expect to turn up?

I've heard that about 25 people have signed up for this course so far, which is pretty good since it's not scheduled until November 15th. I'm expecting a mixture of movie buffs, the curious and the sceptical. But it'll be a great day's *craic*!

Chapter 19

The Sick Squid You Owe Me

Blog by Allen on 1 October 2008
Of Jedi Celebrities and *Star Wars* Actors

You know you've made the big time when a piece about you appears in the North and South Belfast News website. A feature article entitled *Carving Out A Path To Creativity For All* asks some personal questions of yours truly, who it describes as 'South Belfast's most photographed guest lecturer'. Accolades don't come much bigger than this.

Meanwhile, in a galaxy not too far away…

I've had the pleasure of some correspondence recently with a real celebrity and a real gentleman, Gerald Home. Gerald was thoughtful enough to leave an encouraging comment on one of my previous blogs and we've emailed a bit since then. He is originally from Northern Ireland, and played a few characters in *Return of the Jedi*, which is fairly awesome as far as claims to fame go. Heck, the guy even has his own entry in Wikipedia! Visit his website to find out.

What Gerald told me was that there is due to be a sort of *Star Wars* convention at W5 in the Odyssey this weekend. Actually, the event is called Knights of the Empire, and is run by a people who like to dress up as *Star Wars* characters. It will be attended by Gerald and other actors, such as David Prowse (that's the guy who played the physical form of Darth Vader, you idiot). It's on over Saturday and Sunday; I plan to be there on Saturday morning.

But somehow, despite the write-up by Belfast Media, I don't think I'll be signing too many autographs. See you there?

Chapter 20
A Cosm(et)ic Encounter

Blog by Allen on 6 October 2008
A Weekend with the Stars

Last Thursday I was casually informed by a (very pleasant and professional) Press Officer of Queen's University that UTV Life wanted me on Friday. It was to involve a 'sofa chat' with local presenter Frank Mitchell.

Although it was my course on Jedi Training that sparked off their interest in me, the context was the big 'Knights of the Empire' event at the Odyssey at the weekend. The show was due to go out live on Friday 3rd between 5:30 and 6 pm. I landed in the studio just before five in the pm and plunked myself down in the plush foyer, feigning Jedi-like serenity. Then who walked in but David Prowse!

I gulped and went over to introduce myself. Apparently he was due to be on the same time as me. Which was great, because I knew that all the attention would be – rightly – focused on him and therefore deflected from me. As we both sat in make-up together – as one does – his Holywood yarns and friendly manner soon calmed me down.

The interview itself was over in a flash. I think I opened my mouth twice. Other than that I just tried to sit there, looking cool and avoiding the camera's gaze. I did avoid disaster though when I discovered from the autocue that they were going to introduce me as Professor Allen Baird! Someone at Queen's might have had my head for that blip, so I got them to change it to humble Dr instead. But I see that this mistake is still on the UTV website, so I'll enjoy my fantasy promotion while I may...

On Saturday I went to the Knights of the Empire event. Although the costumers were most impressive, the highlight of my day was the opportunity to have lunch with Gerald Home, though he was greatly in demand.

His talk was superb; the audience lapped in all his stories, insights and musings about all *things Star Wars*. He introduced us to the *Star Wars* Outer Rim Alliance. All in all, a very enjoyable experience. But I'm looking forward to chill-out time *this* weekend, so if you want me on your TV or radio show, you'll have to use the Force...

Chapter 21

Me Versus George Lucas, Apparently

Classified Information – FYEO

Email correspondence between Allen and a representative of the feature documentary, The People vs George Lucas.

On Wed, Oct 15, 2008 at 9:27 PM, Allen Baird wrote:

Hello [representative from Quark Films]

My name is Allen Baird. I'm the guy who's delivering the *Feel the Force: How to Train in the Jedi Way* workshop at Queen's University, Belfast.

I've been told that you work for Quark Films and that you want to speak to me about this course. Thanks for the interest.

There has been quite an explosion of interest in this course since the initial university literature was published, but you're the first person from a film company to contact me!

In case you're not aware of it, I've blogged extensively about my media exposure through this course. I'll supply you with the links now, as they might prove useful to you.

I would be delighted to talk with you and give you whatever other information you might need. But I am rather intrigued – as you might expect – as to what you're going to do with it. May I ask what you have in mind?

Give me some ideas about your direction, and if I can help further I'll be only too glad to give you a call and have a chat.

Best regards

Allen

On Mon, Oct 20, 2008 at 9:50 PM, Allen Baird wrote:

Hello [representative from Quark Films]

This is all very interesting! Thanks for the background information and links.

It's a pity that you couldn't be around to film my workshop. The blogging that's gone on about it by the fans has astounded me. I've been on radio stations in Australia and Denmark!

I hadn't planned to have my workshop recorded, but I'm having second thoughts now. If I went ahead and organized this, do you think there would be a chance of its getting included in the production? I guess you can't absolutely guarantee anything, but if I thought this was likely, I think I'd get it recorded and send you a copy, plus maybe a few interviews. Or maybe the interviews themselves would do. What do you think?

Could I ask a few basic questions? Is this a UK or US thing? What does ol' George himself think of it? Is he involved at all?

I've had a chance recently to meet the REAL Darth Vader myself recently – in fact, I did a TV interview with him.

I've also had a run-in with the Jedi guys in Wales, who wanted to come to my course and promote their 'religion' for a BBC3 documentary. Although I was initially tempted, my business partner and university had the sense to say no.

Thanks again for getting in touch. I look forward to your reply.

And, for the record, I'm a 34 year old *mild Star Wars* fan who is blissfully ignorant of the whole 'expanded universe' thing. If you want good sci-fi, look up to H.P. Lovecraft or Ursula Le Guin (in my opinion).

Best regards

Allen

On Tue, Nov 4, 2008 at 9:20 PM, Allen Baird wrote:

Hi [representative from Quark Films], frankly, things are not going well. The people from the Queen's University Media Studies Department have not been helpful, to say the least. They said snootily that they were only into the 'theory' and so were not interested.

I've contacted a few independent, amateur film makers in Northern Ireland but they don't have the right sound equipment. I'm going to phone one of the lecturers tomorrow morning to try and get a definite answer. Surely there must be someone out there who'd be only too happy to get involved in such a project? It's hard to understand their apathy!

I'll get back to you soon.

Thanks for your continued interest and support.

Allen

On Thu, Nov 6, 2008 at 3:35 PM, Allen Baird wrote:

[Representative from Quark Films], good news, I've got someone to do the recording for me! He's a friend of someone in the Queens Sci-fi Club, with his own equipment etc. I'm meeting him soon to sort out the details.

I'll keep you up-to-date with more info as I get it.

Allen

On Thu, Nov 13, 2008 at 7:09 PM, Allen Baird wrote:

[Representative from Quark Films], all is a-ok and good to go. The guy who is doing the filming seems to know what he's about. We met for a coffee on Monday to discuss equipment and I went through what you said. He has a lapel mic and all the right stuff. So we're going to record some of the main parts of the workshop and then do some interviews with me afterwards. Then I'll send it off and you can edit it however you want. As for the university, my new policy is to deal with them as little as possible and just go ahead and organise things myself!

I'll give you a run down after Saturday.

Allen

On Mon, Nov 17, 2008 at 9:04 AM, Allen Baird <allen@sensei-winbeforehand.co.uk> wrote:

Hello XXXX. The workshop went brilliantly, so much so that I'm going to run another one in the spring term! I've got the tapes in my office now. How do I get them to you? Is there an address I can send them to?

Thanks.

Allen

Chapter 22

Foreplay with Hamlet

Their respective abodes.
Friday 14 November 2008

Allen

It's after teatime on a Friday night but no partying for me. I've an early rise in the morning. The class starts at nine thirty in the AM; I aim to be there when the doors open at nine. I iron my favourite, well-worn shirt, the closest I can come to 'smart but casual' without spending a ton. My own fair hands cut my own fair hair. Nails are severed. I do an inventory of my kit.

All video clips and animation on PowerPoint working. Check.

Presentation saved to memory stick. Check.

Training manuals with summaries, diagrams and activities. Check.

University health and safety bumph. Check.

Spare paper and pens. Check.

Evaluation forms printed and packed. Check.

Company flyers and business cards. Check.

Subject-relevant books for students to flick through. Check.

Bottle of water. Check.

Mints. Check.

Wallet, glasses case (plus glasses) and folding umbrella. Check.

Press releases for journalists. Check.

The Force. Check. But it's with me always, anyway, so.

I'm about to teach the UK's first university course on how to be a Jedi. One question: How the feck did that happen?

Give me your answers in the morning. I'm off to bed.

That it should come to this!

Mark

To go or not to go, that is the question.

Whether 'tis nobler in the mind to suffer the flings and hangovers of outrageous boredom or to take arms against a sea of soap operas and by opposing, delay them somewhat.

I can't decide *what condition my condition is in*. It'll depend how I wake up tomorrow morning.

Let's see what old Edward De Bono would say.

On the *plus* side, it gets me out of bed, meeting people and using my brain again.

On the *minus* side, it gets me out of bed, meeting people and using my brain again.

So they basically cancel each other out. That always happens with me when it comes to decision-making. I'm left with a big, fat zero every time.

In the *interesting* column, I'd put, I don't know, I'm curious to evaluate the nerd factor present. That's one point. I've got a hope that some will come dressed in *Star Wars* gear so I can laugh in their faces. That's maybe another point, although it's kind of related to the first. I want to see what this Dr Baird looks like, I'd guess a combination of *Zee Zee Top* and *Dennis Pennis* if such a monstrosity could exist. As long as he doesn't wear a bow-tie and bang on about what a genius George Lucas is - that's the main thing. If George Lucas is so smart then how come he's not Stephen Spielberg then? Answer me that!

So I'm left with no reasons for, none against, but a few reasons why I might want to go if I can be bothered.

Sod it, I'll go.

If its crap I've got the whole Saturday in front of me to visit the off-license, steal into a cinema and get mutely irrigated with horizontal lubricant.

'Tis a consummation devoutly to be wished, so it is.

Chapter 23

Sic et Non

Another generic classroom, Queen's University, Belfast.
Saturday 15 November 2008, 9:34.

"Good morning folks, my name is Dr Baird, or Allen if you're so inclined, please listen up to this health and safety shit the university makes me tell you. What am I, an air hostess? Watch this, its today's first task."

At least that's what I think he says. Or what he should have said.

The first thing he does is show us a *YouTube* clip called *The Jedi Gym*. It's about an American guy who thinks he's a Jedi Master and teaches students to believe in themselves or some such snivelling philosophy, using only the power of their plastic sabers, of course. Then the real Darth Vader comes in and massacres them all. I know how he feels – Vader that is, the treacherous dog – and I am tempted to follow suit. Allen thinks the clip is hilarious. A few of the others seem to agree. I wouldn't know. Let's all have a shaky start then shall we?

And I don't know what I expected him to look like. Probably to be wearing a Jedi bathrobe or something. Instead, he's in jeans and a black shirt with a high collar and open cuffs. I guess it's the most Jedi he can possibly look with a straight face. Doubly so on a cold Saturday morning like this.

As for the rest of him, he's a little under six feet tall, medium build, brown hair cut short, so far just like the majority of us. He has a goatee that hints at the exotic but not by very much. His nose is large and his eyebrows bushy; he could pass for a semi-Arab if his skin was anything but a pasty Irish pale. His voice is soft but he's learned how to project it somehow. They must teach this in Lecturer College along with How To Try To Dress Cool Even Though You're In Your Mid-to-late-thirties. His eye colour seems to shift from a light brown to a dark golden-green.

I purposely arrive just on time so I don't have to engage in any small talk or rumble an excuse. I'm here to know myself but remain unknown to others, as Johari and his Window would say. I'm seated near the front. I take out my mini recorder and switch it on. Also, I switch on my sneer of choice. I think I may have need of it.

"So, there's three big questions you've got to face today. Why is he doing a wacky course like this in the first place? How seriously are we supposed to take all this Jedi stuff? What's the course going to involve?

"First, though, who am I? I am a business and management trainer, unbelievable but true. I am also a tutor here at Queen's

University, Belfast. I teach in the Schools of Education and Management mainly, but I'm also a study skills coach and mental health mentor with QUB Student Support. Out in the real world, I teach stuff like Assertiveness, Body Language, Communication Skills, Positive Psychology, Emotional Intelligence, Confidence Building, Influencing Skills, Decision-making and Time Management. This whole field is usually called soft skills, people skills or meta-skills. Maybe personal and professional development is better?

"Why did I design *this* course? I'd describe myself as a minor *Star Wars* fan. I collected the figures as a boy, and now my favourite t-shirt is one of a storm trooper with a surfboard. What I want to do today is make learning fun, as clichéd as that sounds. Also, I wanted to get more of the male species into my classes, which has worked a little.

"Today started as a daydream, literally. Let's see how it goes.

"Beware as we proceed. This is an experiment in progress. You probably know more than me about *Star Wars*. I'm open to good feedback as we go along with plenty of questions and discussion. So as today evolves please, think about stuff you would like included that isn't, whether the whole idea of 'Jedi training' has a future, and how you would teach it if it was up to you.

"The 'big question' we need to face at the very start of the day: how seriously are we supposed to take all this Jedi stuff?

"I've got two good answers. The first one is, not very seriously. Why? The Jedi are not real. *Star Wars* is a movie for kids. And 'Jediism' is not a religion.

"The Jedi are not real. Get over it! George Lucas himself

103

said, 'The secret to film is that it's an illusion.' And despite some brilliant attempts to project *Star Wars* into our history, we know it's only for fun.[2]

"Some criticise *Star Wars* for being infantile, childish, but let's face the truth - it was made for the age range of adolescence. Someone described it as a space fantasy with the emphasis on interstellar swashbuckling, and with romantic mush kept to a minimum.[3] It therefore appeals to the 8 to 12-year-old boy in all of us. And the thing about it is – it still does.

"In my opinion, 'Jediism' is not a religion. There is no ancient text or tradition. It has no unique revelation or insight. It lacks a special teacher or leader. There is none of the usual religious rituals, never mind a sophisticated worldview or philosophy. But it may become a religion in the future for all I know.

"Having said that, there are several websites that make it out to be a religion. I'll put them up on the screen here. Look at them and see what you think.[4] Or, if you've got a sense of humour, go to YouTube and look up *'Star Wars* Jedi Church' instead.[5]

"Plus, remember that in the first film, *A New Hope*, several of the characters did refer to the word 'religion' with reference to belief in and use of the Force. General Motti chided Vader for his 'sad devotion to that ancient religion.' Han Solo warned Luke that 'hokey religions and ancient weapons are no match for a good

[2] http://www.ifstarwarswasreal.com
[3] Jim Emerson, *How 'Star Wars' Shook the World*
[4] http://www.jedi-church.com/; http://www.jedichurch.org/; http://rumielf.roxer.com/jedihome; http://jediorderofamerica.org/default.aspx; http://leisuresouplarry.googlepages.com
[5] http://www.youtube.com/watch?v=Y2i764rMDfM&feature=related

blaster at your side.' Tarkin tells Vader that he's all that's left of 'that religion.'

"Which takes us into the second answer to the question of how seriously we should take this stuff - fairly seriously. Why? Well, you're probably aware of the famous Jedi census. And don't forget either that *Star Wars* was a groundbreaking film, one that has had a significant cultural impact at that. Most importantly, it somehow speaks to us at a 'deeper level'.

"According to Wikipedia - the source of all true knowledge - the 'Jedi census phenomenon' was a grassroots movement that evolved in 2001 campaigning for citizens in a few English-speaking countries to record their religion as 'Jedi' or 'Jedi Knight' on the national census.

"The campaign was loosely organized by circulating e-mails claiming that if enough people entered 'Jedi,' it would be recognised as an official religion by their government. The emails also implored people to report their religion as Jedi, because 'you love *Star Wars*' or 'just to annoy people.'

"I must admit here that I was one of the weirdoes that said my religion was Jedi. I did it out of anger really. I don't think it's any of the government's business what religion its citizens are. So there. I was vaguely aware that others were doing it but I didn't feel part of a movement or anything like that. Actually, I was slightly worried that the police would arrest me for disrespecting the government or something.

"Australian *Star Wars* Appreciation Society president Chris Brennan did report to *The New Zealand Herald* that while a minority were 'true hard-core people that would believe the Jedi religion carte blanche, the majority of self-reported Jedi claimed the

105

religion for their own amusement, or to poke fun at the government.' That tallies with my experience.

"And the results? In England and Wales 390,127 people (0.7 percent) stated their religion as Jedi on their 2001 Census forms, surpassing Sikhism, Judaism, and Buddhism, and making it the fourth largest reported religion in the country. The highest percentages of such responses were typically in cities with high student populations. In the 2001 Census 2.6 percent of the population of Brighton claimed to be Jedi. That's a whole lot of people!

"Don't forget either that *Star Wars* was a groundbreaking film that changed the movies forever. There was the use of state-of-the-art special effects and surround sound. It created the modern franchise picture and the model for the modern major movie trilogy. It proved you could have a blockbuster hit with *no stars*. My favorite fact: it mixed the genres of science fiction, the Western, the war film, and the quasi-mystical epic. And it served to legitimize comic-book movies, with happy endings.

"And the music was so cool. There's a clip that for me encapsulates all that is magical and powerful about *Star Wars*. Surely, it is one of the greatest scenes in movie history. It's called 'Binary Sunset or Force Theme by John Williams and it makes me tingle and yearn every single time I hear it.

"*Star Wars* has had a massive cultural impact. *Star Wars* references are deeply embedded in popular culture. References to the main characters and themes of *Star Wars* are casually made in many English-speaking countries with the assumption that others will understand the reference.

"Public interest group critics of the Reagan administration's

Strategic Defense Initiative deridingly referred to the orbital missile defense project as *'Star Wars.'* In October 2007, NASA launched a space shuttle carrying an original lightsaber into orbit. The prop handle had been used as Luke Skywalker's in *The Return of the Jedi*. After spending two weeks in orbit, it was brought back to Earth on the seventh of November, 2007, to be returned to its owner, George Lucas.

"Have you heard of 'Project Jedi?' This was an alleged project undertaken by the United States military in the late 1970s to create a super soldier that would possess superior strength, intelligence, cunning, and intuition by utilising *neuro-linguistic programming* techniques. It is thought to have been conducted at Fort Bragg under the United States Army Special Operations Command. It is not specifically known when the program began or if it has ended.

"What is this 'deeper level' at which *Star Wars* speaks to us? We have a story with timeless motifs, a hero that fits a universal pattern, and themes that seem relevant today. More than all that, it provides an ethical reality-check and hints towards spiritual possibilities.

"What are these motifs? The same ones that inhabit fairy stories, nursery rhymes and kids' cartoons since forever. A magical sword. An old, wise mentor. A dark knight. An evil sorcerer. A princess who needs rescuing. An orphan who doesn't know who he is or the power he possesses. A tyrannical empire. A small band of goodies fighting against seemingly overwhelming odds.

"All this fits a pattern. Lucas was influenced by a scholar and author called Joseph Campbell. He developed a version of mythology that's called The Hero's Journey, the heroic monomyth.

This basic pattern forms the story arc of most mythological tales. It's based in part on the work of Jung, who wrote about the archetypes of the collective unconscious, like the wise old man and the hero. This is the root of every culture's storytelling, a common psychological pool from which every storyteller draws, whether beside a fire or in front of a screen.

"First there is the call to adventure, with the possibility of a helper (think of Luke Skywalker called by R2D2, and assisted by Obi Wan Kenobi and the robots).

"Second there is the threshold crossing, with tests and more helpers (the death of Luke's aunt and uncle, and the appearance of more helpers - Hans Solo and Chewbacca).

"Third there is the supreme ordeal (Luke's confrontation with his father, Darth Vader). Fourth there is the return, with a possible boon to the hero's people (Luke destroys the Death Star, the rebel alliance is saved).

"We'll look at these in more depth later.

"The relevant themes are a matter of opinion, in this case, my opinion. We have the problem of a planet-destroying weapon. We have a man who is half a machine. We have a call to trust instinct instead of technology. We have the political problems raised by civil disobedience against perceived tyranny. Rebels versus imperials, or separatists versus republicans, it's a matter of perspective.

"Ethics is important in *Star Wars*. According to another author, George Lucas aimed to restore notions of good and evil, with the idea of heroes and villains. Vietnam had complicated and relativised these concepts, but Lucas wanted to revive them. Why else do you think the baddie soldiers are called Storm Troopers?

"And from ethics, we move on to spirituality. We've heard recently in the news about the Large Hadron Collider. According to our old friend Wikipedia, here are some of the questions that this piece of equipment is meant to help us answer. Are electromagnetism, the strong nuclear force and the weak nuclear force just different manifestations of a *single unified force*, as predicted by various Grand Unification Theories? What is the nature of *dark matter and dark energy*? Are there *extra dimensions*, as predicted by various models inspired by string theory, and can we detect them?

"It's hard for a *Star Wars* fan not to read stuff into this!

"So, finally, what are we going to cover today?

"I've split up our Jedi training into four sections.

"First, following this introduction, there's your initiation into Jedi training. I'll do this by testing your Force sensitivity. Next, we're going to follow the rise of Luke as a full Jedi Knight as he develops his skills of Force flow, Force influence and Force control. Then, we'll trace Anakin's tragic downfall from the Jedi way, as he leaves the way of balance, mindfulness and detachment. Finally, I want to go back to the hero's journey in order to provide you with a pattern for your own Jedi adventure.

"There are many topics I'd love to attempt in a course like this, but I don't feel that I'm qualified to do so. My essential training lies in the tradition of Western philosophy and psychology. I am unable to cover possibly relevant topics like meditation, sword skills, or Eastern tactics of 'mind control' and the so-called 'warrior philosophy'.

"On top of this, I can think of other topics I'm tempted to cover but we're not able to due to lack of time. The psychology of the shadow or 'dark side' of human nature. Mediation and negotiation skills. How to increase your bodily senses and agility. An examination of the philosophies of power and technology. Developing mental strength in empathy, intuition, courage and resourcefulness. Even theories to do with the 'father wound.' It's all there. But for later.

"Right now, let's start with that initiation. First thing after a break."

Here endeth his first lesson. Coffee or death awaits.

For the moment, I choose coffee.

Chapter 24

A Gaping Void

The same generic classroom, Queen's University, Belfast.
Saturday 15 November 2008, 11:06.

"If someone called you 'sensitive', would you take it as a compliment?"

After teasing us with this one, Baird now shows us a cartoon by a guy called Hugh MacLeod. Apparently, MacLeod does drawings on the back of business cards. If this is anything to go by, clearly they rock, I must confess.

It's a picture of a post-modern hippie type, male, complete with ragged goatee and shades. The speech bubble from his mouth says, "Hi, I'm the 'sensitive-but-manly' type who likes to think the sun shines out of his ass..."

I wonder if Dr Baird realises just how close he comes to fulfilling this stereotype himself. He certainly has the beard. But his hair is shorter, smacking a little of the military buzz-cut. He probably harbours delusions of soldierhood, in the army cadets as a boy but never quite had the stones to join up. You know the type, can recite the difference in bullet calibre between the M-16 and the AK-47 but never made it onto the school football team.

As for myself, I make a point of never wearing sunglasses unless I'm driving with the light in my eyes. It makes me feel superior, especially to people who push them on to the top of their heads when they go indoors. This is the second surest sign of an A1 asshole. The first? An adult fascination with *Star Wars*.

Here we go again.

"In the *Star Wars* universe, the Jedi are one major group of people who have Force abilities. Those who do are called Force-sensitive.

"And I quote. 'A Force-sensitive was a being who was highly attuned to the flow of the Force. Force-sensitives could, with training, learn to sense and manipulate the Force.'[6]

"Jedi can sense the Force and the world of the Force. They are aware of things that others are not. In the later films, we're told that this was due to the presence of midi-chlorians, microscopic life forms that live within our cells and link sentient beings with the Force. Only a minority of individuals possess them. This minority are the Force-sensitives, Jedi, Sith and others.

"What if I were to tell you that there are a minority of human beings in this world, in this classroom, who possess a similar sensitivity? In 1999, a respected psychotherapist called Elaine Aron wrote a book called *The Highly Sensitive Person*. In it, she

---

[6] http://starwars.wikia.com/wiki/Force-sensitive

claims to have discovered a class of humans whose nervous system is more sensitive to subtleties than average. Their sight, hearing, and sense of smell are not necessarily keener, although they may be. But their brains' processes information differently and reflect on it more deeply than others. She says that this trait is inherited by 15% to 20% of the population.

"Being a Highly Sensitive Person or 'HSP' also means, necessarily, that you are more easily over stimulated, stressed out, and overwhelmed than others. Unless, that is, you learn to control and use it to your advantage. It has often been mislabeled as many things. Some confuse it with shyness, which is not an inherited trait. Others identify it with introversion, whereas 30% of HSPs are actually extraverts. Many label themselves as inhibited, fearful, and the like. Aron claims instead that it is a great gift.

"If you are an HSP, you have special powers. You are aware of details in your surroundings, such as the moods and personalities of others. You have greater powers of imagination, empathy, creativity and insight. You are the first one to perceive when something needs done in a crisis. You possess greater intuition to 'just know' without realising how. You give more care and reflection when processing information than others. You have the ability to make finer distinctions between things, emotions, concepts, categories, perspectives than others make.

"There are real mental differences involved here. HSP's are better at spotting errors and avoiding making errors. They are able to concentrate deeply. They excel at tasks requiring vigilance, accuracy, speed, and the detection of subtle differences. They are able to process information at deeper levels of 'semantic memory.' They are skilled at thinking about our own thinking – what psychologists call 'metacognition'. They often learn without being aware that they have learned. They are deeply affected by other people's moods and emotions.

"These differences spill out into the realm of the body too. HSP's may be good at holding still, or specialists at fine motor movements. They may find themselves more sensitive to things in the air. They get more stimulated by things like caffeine unless very used to them. In general, HSP's possess greater receptivity to sensory stimulation than non-sensitives.

"I am a Highly Sensitive Person.

"How do I know? I could give you anecdotal evidence about my sensitivity to perfume and animal fur, my pain sensitivity, how I get overwhelmed with noise and bustle, the way music brings me to tears in a second, my inability to multi-task, my enjoyment of delicate or fine scents, tastes, sounds, works of art. I am affected by the moods of others, and perform badly while observed. Certain small noises can drive me mad. My inner life is rich and complex – IMHO! – and my ability for self-reflection has been described by a university lecturer as profound. People would probably classify me a quiet and calm, but this is an external mask I have created to deal with the world.

"Does any of this sound familiar to you? If so, you may be Highly Sensitive too. But don't go by stories alone. Aron has developed a test.[7] Take it now; search for the midi-chlorians in you!

"If you come up short, don't worry, we'll allow you to stay.

---

[7] http://www.hsperson.com/pages/test.htm

If you pass, congratulations! You are now ready to start your training. As the man said, 'You've taken your first step into a larger world!'"

Or the first step into a waste of a £28 and a Saturday morning.

Still, at least we're getting a bit of substance now, a bit of the psychological stuff. I hadn't heard of this HSP concept before, and if anyone had called me the sensitive type, I'd have tested the sensitivity of their throat against the space between the index finger and thumb of my left hand. Violence pays. That's the sole moral I can dredge from Northern Ireland's sad history, at least that I can think of.

I take the test.

Ah. It turns out that I'm an HSP too, along with half the class, which says something about either the class or the test, I don't know which.

I approve of belonging to a biological elite. Not in a fascist sense, you understand, way too *herd* for me.

But it does suit my view of the world. It seems rather *un*Jedi though. Aren't they all for equality and other forms of sentimental do-goodery? Maybe altruism is based on a superiority complex as I've always suspected: I look down on him; therefore I can reach down to help him.

Maybe I'm about to find out.

Chapter 25

Chicks Send Me High

The same generic classroom, Queen's University, Belfast.
Saturday 15 November 2008, 12:01.

He wants to mash in a bit more training before lunch. About time, feeding time that is.

On with it, then, Jedi Master. Set out your wares. Impress me with your insights. Otherwise the class will be missing one more stomach after lunch, and not because of the intellectual mind-fest I've just received. The Jedi are monks after all. Maybe our mystical sensei is on the mental equivalent of bread-and-water today. But I need some meat. I'm a carnivore.

Impress me, make me salivate.

"There are three lessons from the life of Luke that we're going to use as a model for our own Jedi training. In each of these situations, Luke confronts something monstrous. For each, he

116

needs a particular Jedi ability in order to complete his mission.

"First, when faced with the Death Star, he required 'flow'. Next, when communicating Jabba the Hutt, he used 'assertiveness'. Finally, in the presence of Darth Vader, ultimately overcoming the Emperor, Luke relied on 'control' rather than his lightsaber.

"Let's look at these in turn.

"From the commencement, Ben Kenobi tells Luke that a Jedi can feel the Force flowing through him. According to Master Yoda, the basis of Jedi Strength is their ability to draw on the 'flow' of the Force, hardly a simple task. It is much easier to draw from the dark-side of fear and anger. Their flow of strength is rapid, especially in a situation of fight or flight. However once you begin to use their power, you become a flow instrument or 'slave' rather than a 'master' or wielder of flow.

"Let me ask you a question. Have you ever felt like this? You feel completely 'at one' with what you are doing so that you become a verb, a doing thing. You know you are strong and able to control your destiny, at least in that moment. You gain an immediate sense of pleasure independent of longer-term results or goals. You lose track of time because you're engrossed.

"I experience this in two circumstances. Chiefly, I experience it when I'm studying, engrossed in research material and ideas. This might occur when I'm preparing to teach a class or writing something for a journal. To a lesser extent, I feel it when I jog. The first marathon I participated in – I only ran part of it in case you're impressed – I had trained hard. On the day I was completely ready and focused. Once I started, I tuned in to my body and legs, which just means I concentrated on every movement to the exclusion of everything else. I don't refer to anything mystical

117

here, only focus, on the rhythm, on the road, on my breathing. I became what I can only describe as 'a running thing'. My existence was reduced to the sole activity of running and nothing else. That's what I meant by becoming a verb.

"Psychologists call this experience 'flow' or optimal experience. Let's look at Wikipedia. 'Flow' is a mental state of operation in which the person is fully immersed in what he or she is doing, characterized by a feeling of energized focus, full involvement, and success in the process of the activity. Proposed by psychologist Mihaly Csikszentmihalyi, the concept has been widely referenced across a variety of fields. These areas include sports, education and learning, music, and meditation.

"Flow is so named because during Csikszentmihalyi's 1975 interviews several people described their 'flow' experiences using the metaphor of a current carrying them along. Many modern sports people commonly experience this phenomenon, referring to it as *being in the zone*. The psychological concept of *flow* as becoming absorbed in an activity is therefore unrelated to the older phrase 'to go with the flow' which means 'to conform.'

"Think of flow as a mental state between tedium and trauma, apathy and anxiety. In any task, two factors are present: the challenge of the task or how difficult it is; and, the skills you possess to accomplish it. If I told you to lift a pencil off the desk, this is both low challenge and low skill. The result? Apathy. If I now gave you the task of calculating pi to the hundredth decimal place, I guess most of us would not have the skills to cope. It would create anxiety. If I gave you the task of doing what you do to relax, you might be able to do this easily, even if it required a high degree of skill. But if that was all you were allowed to do forever, you'd

118

eventually get bored. Any sense of changing challenge would be absent.

"Flow happens in our minds as the levels of challenge and skill coincides and grows together. It therefore requires high challenge and high skill relative to where we're starting from. To know where you go for flow, ask yourself, what is my favorite activity? This does not mean the one that gives you the easiest gratification. Usually, it's the one that makes you feel most absorbed, in which you can claim some degree of 'unconscious competence.'

"What was it for Luke? Piloting, I think. He was a skilled pilot before he became a Jedi. He longed to develop his flying skills at the academy, and to use these skills in the cause of the Rebellion. It was his ability to experience flow that enabled him to destroy the Death Star in his X-Wing. He used the Force to aid his concentration and order his consciousness rather than the electronic targeting device. He had mastered flow.

"You think I've made this up? Listen to the words of Professor Martin Seligman. 'Role models and paragons in the culture compellingly illustrate a strength or virtue. Models may be real (Mahatma Ghandi and humane leadership), apocryphal (George Washington and honesty), or explicitly mythic (Luke Skywalker and flow).'[8] A role model is a role model, fictional or not. The skill and the experience are real. That is what matters.

"If you will become a Jedi Knight, you must find and use

---

[8] Martin Seligman, *Authentic Happiness*, p. 138

your sense of flow. You must be able to recognise it and produce it when in need! Use this description from Wikipedia to find your flow. Discuss it with your fellow padawans."

Oh the pain, the pain, the groupwork, the pain, the pain.

I can sense those sitting around me glancing at each other, trying to smile. It's like standup for puritans. I stare straight ahead, at the Wikipedia rip-off he's put on the screen.

Here's what it says.

How the experts describe flow experiences
- *Clear goals* (expectations and rules are discernable)
- *Concentrating and focusing*, a high degree of concentration on a limited field of attention (a person engaged in the activity will have the opportunity to focus and to delve deeply into it)
- A *loss of the feeling of self-consciousness*, the merging of action and awareness
- *Distorted sense of time* - our subjective experience of time is altered
- Direct and immediate *feedback* (successes and failures in the course of the activity are apparent, so that behavior can be adjusted as needed)
- *Balance between ability level and challenge* (the activity is neither too easy nor too difficult)
- A sense of personal *control* over the situation or activity
- The activity is *intrinsically rewarding*, so there is an effortlessness of action

As I read it, two suggestions come immediately to mind.

Suddenly I decide that discretion is the better part of valour. Better to play the game than moan from the sidelines, and all that. Anyway, I want to hear what these saddos have to say for themselves. I turn my chair around 180 degrees and hey-presto I've formed my own group.

A guy who looks like a Dutch exchange student starts to talk aimlessly.

"It's like my computer time? Especially at night? When I'm sitting in front of my computer? It's like, I become one with my computer, you know?"

Oh no, I think. Please don't start to talk about pornography. Please.

Then I think, on second thoughts do, I want to watch the rest of them squirm.

So I ask him what me means.

"C plus plus. Java. C sharp. You name it man, I do it. I think, like, when I'm in that groove, like, it's if I'm breathing air or whatever?"

He's clearly breathing something. I'm trying to figure out if C plus plus is a bra size I haven't heard of when someone else in the group, a rather prim, middle aged lady, tries to untie the Gordian knot.

"You're a computer programmer."

"Yea, yea. When I'm writing code, I don't notice the time going down. I want to stay there forever. I'm coding deeper and deeper. My fingers merge with the keyboard. I don't care what's going on round me. It's the flow, like, the flow, sort of thing."

Good grief and other oxymorons.

The others try to chip in. One mentions hockey, the other,

Sudoku. They make my two initial thoughts – sex and the art of copious alcohol consumption – seem like touches of genius. Instead, I practice my lying.

"Sometimes, when I'm climbing a mountain, all my focus is on my next move, arm or foot. It's like physical chess, me against the mountain. I forget how cold I am, how tired, how alone. I don't think about what I'll do that night, who I'll be with. I don't even think about my own name. Just the next half a metre. Body, brain and will all working in harmony. Using every ounce of skill I have, every previous experience. The alpine scenery melts into the background. It's up to me and no one else. A beautiful thing."

They look improbably impressed, all of them. It's all I can do to stop myself taking it to the next level. You know, *then sometimes it starts to snow and I'm trapped out there all night* sort of thing, but being a good liar is as much about knowing when to quit as anything else. So I do.

They yap on a bit about reading mostly, reading a French novel, reading a scientific journal, and of course, reading computer code. Apparently, this constitutes their idea of a challenge. Action figures they are not.

The closest they attain to any high-octane exploit is watching MacGyver on satellite TV. I would have shat myself if one of them had mentioned mountaineering and asked me to expand, but no fear of that among this collection of shrinking violetta.

Still, all comedy aside, I do feel something like this when I write. Flow, I mean, not shatting.

Dr Baird asks for our examples. Our group tells him "computer programming."

122

He strives to look gratified for their non-insightful contribution.

For the first time today, I allow myself a Duchenne smile. Pan-Am can fly with the crows.

Chapter 26

Majordomo Zero

The same generic classroom, Queen's University, Belfast.
Saturday 15 November 2008, 12:27.

This is the last round before lunch, so he tells us. Then I'm off for a few rounds of my own, on my own.

I want this section to really suck so I won't feel guilty about quitting at half time. Not that guilt is an issue for me. I've given it up for lent.

Still, I might have that nagging feeling that I've missed out, that there was some afternoon gem that escaped my grasp. So far, the decision is on a knife-edge, unfortunately, only in a metaphorical sense.

This will be the test.

"If I had to capture it in one word, I would say that the way of the Jedi is the way of assertiveness. Assertiveness is the path between dark-side aggression and weak-minded passivity. The Jedi are warrior-monks. They take the strength of the warrior and the control of the monk. The way of life produced by this union is called the assertive life.

"What is assertiveness? Literally, it means *'forceful'*! Assertiveness is usually defined as the art of clear, direct communication. If you assert yourself, you behave in a way that expresses your power over yourself and for yourself, as well as with and from others. But you achieve this in a way that allows others their power too. Usually it occurs in relation to a personal need or where you consider that rational argument or debate is inappropriate or irrelevant. Assertive techniques are one of the main forms of influence – along with arguing, empathising and energising.

"Although many film viewers and non-Jedi don't realise it, Luke employs a number of assertiveness techniques in his tense confrontation with Jabba to rescue Han Solo. This is where a careful reading of the script is essential. To movie watchers, it seems that Luke uses a standard Jedi mind-trick to influence Bib Fortuna (successfully) and then Jabba himself (unsuccessfully at least at the start).

"The script describes the incident in greater detail, adding many vital word-clues. Luke strides purposefully. Luke does not stop. Luke tells Bib what he wants. Luke stops, stares and raises his hand. Luke tells Bib what will happen. When Bib responds, Luke praises him. Luke strares hard at Jabba and makes his demands. He repeats them along with a prediction of what will happen if they are not met. The verbal negotiations are concluded.

"The mystical Jedi mind-trick is one of the most recognisable and borrowed phrases in *Star Wars* lore. But there's a

125

problem with this interpretation. In actual fact, there is little magic here at all. What Luke does is employ a range of standard assertiveness techniques to aid him in his quest. Anyone can learn to use them against the weak-minded!

"First, notice Luke's use of power words. There are individual expressions that exert a great deal of persuasive force upon the human mind. They work both ways – when someone says them to us, or we speak them to another. Chief among these everyday words are 'I' statements. Luke says, "*I* must speak with Jabba... *I* must be allowed to speak... *I* warn you not to underestimate my powers."

"These are among the most powerful statements you can make and are the hallmark of assertive communication. They affirm who you are and what you want. Their impact lies in that they reveal your exact position and expectations. They don't have to guess or negotiate. Other 'power words' are: 'No,' 'When,' and 'If.' Luke uses 'no' too, especially when being tempted to join the dark-side by Vader and the Emperor. He does not question or negotiate in the face of evil; he simply says "no."

"Second, Luke makes a simple statement of request. 'You will bring Captain Solo and the Wookiee to me.' This involves a clear, factual declaration of what you want/don't want, or expect. It sets out your standards, rules, or instructions. You make clear your demands – what you don't want or find acceptable. *This is one of the core assertive openers:* 'I need, I expect, I wish...'

"Third, Luke persists. When Jabba initially refuses, Luke states his position again as a fact. 'Nevertheless, I'm taking Captain Solo and his friends.' This is popular technique advocated by assertiveness experts called *the broken record technique.* It consists

126

of simply repeating your requests every time you are met with illegitimate resistance. The term comes from the vinyl records of the mid twentieth century, the surface of which when scratched would lead the needle of a record player to loop over the same few seconds of the recording indefinitely.

"Fourth, Luke states the consequences. 'You can either profit by this or be destroyed! It's your choice.' In this stage, you specify what will happen to the other person *if* they do not comply with your expectations. This consequence can specify what will happen naturally or by your own application. If the latter, it must be within your control and you must be prepared to follow through. 'If you won't X, I will Y.'

"Fifth, Luke has tremendous control of his body language, or non-verbal communication. The script, and indeed the film, depicts Luke as entirely in control of how he speaks, walks and stands. His voice and eye contact are highly focused. He uses gestures at key moments to backup and increase his words.

"Likewise when we see the Jedi mind-trick used by Obi-Wan in the famous 'these are not the droids you're looking for' scene. Ben speaks in what is described as a 'very controlled voice'. He emphasizes with a hand gesture.

"It astonishes people to learn the power of body language when persuading others. According to one famous statistic, words only account for 7% of our total meaning, while voice tone counts for 38% and body language a whopping 55%. True, this applies mainly when we first meet someone. As we get to know and trust them, the verbal element increases in direct proportion to trust. But the non-verbal elements remain particularly important for communicating *feelings* and attitudes, both to others and to yourself. They are 'silent messages' that experts can read, interpret and employ to advantage.

"A Jedi Knight is able to use his or her body language as a powerful means of influencing the weak-minded.

"You must start to use *your* body-language to reinforce your purposes when dealing with others. What do you think are the signs of assertive body-language?"

Now this is rather more like it, useful, definite. Powerful. I know some of this already because I've read about them. It was a fine overview but thin on detail. Maybe the Jedi aren't the boy-scout schmucks I imagined. I'd like to talk to the Doc about it.

Anyway, at the present we've got another group-work exercise to complete. What are the signs of assertive body language? I turn around again and squash any thoughts of mountaineering. Instead, I think I'll provide a little lesson in assertive behaviour, a real-time case study if you will. I take control.

"Right. Let's make a list of assertive signs. I'll be scribe. Any ideas?"

Not that I wanted their ideas. I have my own and that's enough. But it gets them talking to each other and out of my face. So I get a bit of paper from one of their notebooks and begin to write.

1) **Eye contact - good contact without staring**

2) **Facial expression - interested, steady, relaxed**

3) **Movements & gestures – open, tilted**

4) **Positioning – appropriate distance, pointed**

5) **Stance & posture – upright, still, spacious**

6) **Voice – clear, firm, congruous**

128

By the time the conversation runs dry – which is to say after approximately 23 seconds – I've finished. I read it out.

No point knowing if you're backward showing. I know, I show.

As we leave for lunch, I stop off for a quick work with *herr doktor*.

He's making for his coat – a trendy USA Military Winter Field Jacket – and exchanging eye-contact and a quick nod with a big guy at the back of the room. I deduce that they're off for dinner together. I'd like to further deduce some smutty conclusion from this liaison but they aren't the type, either of them. Body language and all that.

Since I'm slightly smaller than him and slightly smaller than most males there's a move that I do. When I talk to someone standing up I always go a smidgen too close, invade their personal space to a degree enough to cause discomfort, but not enough to make them think I'm a stalker or psycho. It makes them take a step back, physically and therefore psychologically. Puts them on the back foot. I try it here.

It doesn't work. He stands his ground, looking a little down on me. If I could read his mind, if we were telepathic, he would say *I know what you're trying but I've mastered the art of self control so fuck off.* Only I don't think he's a fuck off kind of communicator. That language is too plebian.

Anyway I won't call him 'Allen' or 'Doctor Baird' since I'm neither his playmate nor his patient.

"I want to ask you about something you said."

"Very good, very assertive," he says.

"Yeah. Anyway I was wondering if you think it's

129

manipulative to use these forms of influencing. That doesn't seem very Jedi."

"In a sense using influencing techniques is manipulative. We are using certain skills to control people for our own advantage, no doubt about it. Where I would draw the line is that I remain open to their influence on me. So we use these skills to mutual advantage, at the expense of neither party and for the benefit of both. We use them to seek win-win outcomes, to play an infinite game rather than a zero-sum one."

"And what if the other person doesn't have these skills?" I ask, all innocence.

"I believe that it is their responsibility to acquire them, and my responsibility to teach them. That way we can work towards a level playing field."

"Can the weak-minded ever acquire these skills?" I insist.

"I think so. It's one of my passions and fundamental premises that anyone can acquire any of these skills to some degree. If the teaching is good enough."

"So the weak-minded are weak-minded due to lack of training rather than lack of basic ability?" I enquire.

"I think so. Anyway that's why I'm here today."

"OK thanks," I say, and make to leave.

"Your name's familiar. Have you been to any of my classes before?" he says.

I pause and turn in my tracks.

"Yes. You taught a workshop last year called 'Power-Plays: How to Take Control in Life'. I was sick but asked for the notes."

"Oh. Any good?"

"Life changing."

I walk out leaving him with a confused expression on his face, the eyes squinted, the brow pulled a little down, the head tilted. He doesn't know if I was sarcastic and didn't have time to read my face. He's taught courses on non-verbal communication and lie-detection so he can do all that if given a chance. Body language and all that.

If I had to bet, I'd guess he would conclude that I was using sarcasm to hide the inconvenient truth that it did. Change my life I mean. He'd be spot on. Machiavelli, Nietzsche, Greene, I drunk it all in. And he doesn't even remember me, his prize pupil.

Not that it bothers me; I was only there in the vicarious sense. This perhaps sounds like sour grapes but it's true, that's the godforsaken beauty of it. His class taught me what power is, and how to wield it over my life, over others, and above all over myself. He taught me how to place those things I have no control over into another place, one beyond all concern and anxiety. He taught me to have control over my attitude, responses and motivations. He made me a god. And a god is capable of attaining any goal, managing any situation. In the jargon of his workshop this state was called 'self-efficacy'. I call it omnipotence.

I have the power to come back after lunch, and the power to refrain.

Absolute control.

Holy guacamole I'm ready to collapse with hunger!

Mexican it is then.

Chapter 27

As He Faced the Sun

The same generic classroom, Queen's University, Belfast.
Saturday 15 November 2008, 1:45pm.

There are certain words, I think, that sound like their meanings. No, I don't mean onomatopoeia. I dislike animals, whether they go *quack*, *bleat* or *croak*. And don't get me started on *zap* and *honk*. Or tell me I've had too much to drink over lunch.

Absolute control.

I'm talking about the word 'synchronicity.' Even if you couldn't define it, if you'd never heard it before, you could make a pretty good stab at it. Unless you were proper stupid and didn't even get in to a Grammar School.

Most people know words like *synchronise*, as in the action movie line about watches. Most people know about introverts and extroverts. Most people are tools.

I digress. Synchronicity is a Jungian term, only you don't pronounce the 'j' in the dude's name for some foreign reason. Synchronicity denotes when two events are related by meaning rather than causality.

The last thing I was thinking about in this classroom before lunch was control; the first thing Dr Baird speaks about in this classroom after lunch is control. This is a coincidence beyond chance. But the one thing was not triggered by the other. Except in my head. Hence, synchronicity.

Ah forget it. It's time to start again. Where's that damned recorder?

"'Control' sounds like a boring sort of word. It makes you think of self-control in the sense of not doing anything adventurous, having no ambition, never revealing who you really are. This is not what I mean by control. What I mean is what psychologists call *emotional self-management*, a subset of Emotional Intelligence. I define this as the skill of regulating your emotions and impulses as they occur. A person with this ability can harness emotions and direct them to achieve intended goals and adapt to changing circumstances.

"During the course of the *Star Wars* films, Luke endures several tragedies. He loses his uncle and aunt. His home is destroyed. He has to leave everything he knows. His mentor is murdered. Many of his comrades are killed. His best friend is captured and tortured. His body is mutilated. His newly discovered sister is threatened. And it turns out his main enemy is his father. That's a lot to deal with, even for a Jedi!

"Given all that, it would be easy for dark and negative emotions to overwhelm him. Hatred for his enemies! Fear of what

133

they threaten to all you love! But they do not. Even Darth Vader remarks that Obi-Wan has taught him well. Why? Luke has mastery over his fear. At another point, Yoda explains to Luke that fear and anger are connected. One leads to the other; both result in suffering.

"In assertiveness theory, too, there is a link between anger and fear. Assertiveness is the midpoint between an aggressive outlook and a passive state. Aggression is the belief that you take all the power, only your rights count, if you win others must loose. It is associated with the emotion of anger. The opposite is passivity, a position of fear and timidity. Assertiveness rejects both anger and fear as motives for behavior in favour of equality.

"A Jedi must therefore learn to control two dark-side emotions, or become controlled by them in return. How you control them, the techniques you choose, will differ from from Jedi to Jedi. The main thing is that we try to discover what works for us. Here's what works for me.

"For controlling fear, I learn to separate fantasy from reality in the case of irrational or 'catastrophic' thinking. And I face the consequences of facing my rational fears, for example, by 'contingency planning,' 'risk assessment' or my favourite, Worst Case Scenario thinking. Perhaps most importantly, I learn to control the emotion of fear itself. So I have learned to relax, meditate, and use creative visualisation or breathing techniques. I've used these to overcome my fears of public speaking (as you can now witness) and heights.

"Probably the best advice I can give you on how to be brave comes from two Americans, one a psychologist and the other a politician.

"The first quote is from William James, and the second from Theodore Roosevelt, a most remarkable man. Here's what they said.

"'Action seems to follow feeling, but really action and feeling go together; by regulating the action, which is under the more direct control of the will, we can regulate the feeling, which is not...Thus the sovereign voluntary path to cheerfulness, if our spontaneous cheerfulness be lost, is to sit up cheerfully and to act and speak as if cheerfulness were already there. If such conduct does not make you feel cheerful, nothing else on that occasion can...So, to feel brave, act as if we were brave, use all of our will to that end, and a courage fit will very likely replace the fit of fear.'

"'Having been a rather sickly and awkward boy, I was, as a young man, at first nervous and distrustful of my own prowess. I had to train myself painfully and laboriously not merely as regards my body but as regards my soul and spirit...When a boy I read a passage in one of Marryat's books which always impressed me. In this passage, the captain of some small British man-of-war is explaining to the hero how to acquire the quality of fearlessness.
He says at the outset almost every man is frightened when he goes into action, but that the course to follow is for the man to keep such a grip on himself that he can act just as if he were not frightened.
After this has been kept up long enough, it changes from a pretence to a reality, and the man does in fact become fearless by sheer dint of practising fearlessness when he does not feel it...This is the theory upon which I went.

"'There were all kinds of things of which I was afraid at first, ranging from grizzly bears to 'mean' horses and gun-fighters; but by acting as if I was not afraid I gradually ceased to be afraid.

Most men can have the same experience if they choose.'

"As far as Anger Management is concerned, again, all I can tell you is what works for me. Probably the best way is to learn to express your feelings appropriately and skilfully i.e. by *assertive* communication. We get angry because we remain passive too long and wait until our inner rage explodes. A little assertiveness now prevents a lot of anger later.

"I suggest also to you that you challenge and change your attitude towards anger. See it for it's true nature, for what it is in itself - immature, bestial, easy. Consider these wise words from an ancient master.

"'Anyone can become angry – that is easy. But to be angry with the right person, to the right degree, at the right time, for the right purpose, and in the right way – this is not easy.'[9]

"Face your own 'dark side.' Jung spoke of the *shadow* or *shadow aspect* of human nature. It is a part of the unconscious mind consisting of aspects of ourselves that we have repressed. We do this because we consider them a form of weaknesses or a source of shame. Everyone carries such a dark side with them. The less we acknowledge it in our conscious life, the blacker and more powerful is its hold over us.

"Deal with a backlog of unresolved anger. Deep-seated anger and resentment usually has some specific cause in a person's past. There is no such thing as anger-in-general, only anger-at-something. Discover what this something is. While gratitude is

---

[9] Aristotle, Nicomachean Ethics (II.1109a27)

136

positive emotion about good events in your past, forgiveness is positive emotions about the negative events in your past.

"Forgiveness is difficult but here is how I have learned to think about it and use it to my advantage. I insist that forgiveness is a gift, not a right. I value forgiveness as a sign of the giver's position of strength, not weakness. I remember the need I have of forgiveness and those who have forgiven me. And I realise that vengefulness poisons and controls the one who feels it. It is liberating and powerful to forgive, perhaps the ultimate expression of personal control.

"Find constructive channels for your anger energy, or a positive cause to put it too. Be angry against the evils of oppression and injustice. More specifically, take physical exercise to work out the energy that anger creates. It is hard to be angry and exhausted at the same time.

"Jedi Knights have total control over their emotional state. This is doubly true regarding the negative emotions of fear and anger.

"Have you faced and defeated your fear and anger? Think of a repetitive situation in which they defeat you. How will you now overcome them?"

I get the feeling I'm listening to a sermon here. I can imagine the guy as some sort of minister or youth pastor or whatever they're called these days. He has the twinkle of zealot-eye about him under that new-man exterior.

But an evangelist for what? I'm not sure yet. Personal development? Self-actualisation? A Jedi homeworld? Anyway, I don't like the preaching. All the *forgiveness is good* this, *unresolved anger issues* that. Is this a cross between a revival meeting and group therapy? If there's a difference.

Anger can give you strength, he admitted that himself. It's like a fire burning within, giving out energy, heat, power. You fuel it with all the shit you encounter every day. Yea, that's it, a shit-fueled fire. And there's so much shit, so much to burn. An unlimited supply of deadwood for the furnace. The furnace being me, myself, and my brain. Don't get too close or I'll burn ya!

Hell's bells, I need some water! I always forget to drink when I drink. It's hard to feel controlled when your brain has gone walkabout through the blistering bushland of dehydration.

Good job there's no time for group discussion. He's pressing on with a vengeance.

Me too.

Chapter 28

Kansas Wizardry

The courtyard quad, Queen's University, Belfast.
Saturday 15 November 2008, 2:38 pm

The fire alarm went off for no reason. Fifteen minutes of standing out in the cold helped clear my head a little of gibber-gabber and fill my lungs with unclean air. God gave fags and with rock 'n roll to me.

Are Jedi allowed to get drunk, *that* is the question.

Time is getting a little tight now. But it gives me an excuse to go and shake hands with the president. Liquid goes in, liquid goes out, law of nature.

The dog is turned to his own vomit again; and the sow that was washed to her wallowing in the mire.

I once heard a street preacher quote this at me while what passed for his wife thrust a tract in my face called 'Name 10 Beers'.

So it must be true. However it did strike me as a little immoderate. Excluding brands, no-one knows more than six beer types.

We go back in.

"There are three failures in the life of Anakin that can also aid us in our quest to train as Jedi. In each of three trials, despite his natural powers, Anakin proved an epic failure. This, for me, is very telling. Skill with lightsaber and speeder do not a Jedi make.

"First, there was Anakin's failure to fulfil his destiny in terms of the prophecy. He lacked balance. Second, there was his failure to be aware of his negative thinking style. Anakin lacked mindfulness. Finally, there was his failure to maintain a Jedi sense of selflessness. Detachment was totally lacking. And so his failure was complete.

"Qui-Gon Jinn believed that the birth of Anakin was a fulfillment of prophecy. This prophecy foretold a chosen one who would bring balance to the Force. Qui-Gon's dying command to his apprentice, Obi-Wan, was to train Anakin to fulfill this role. Mace Windu and Yoda were unsure but seemed to accept that it was possible. Later, Yoda seemed to believe that it is Anakin's destiny to bring balance, as long as he chose to follow this path.

"But how do we know which is the right path to follow? Ethics, the study of right and wrong, has given us two solutions: you obey certain laws or you measure certain consequences. These are the ways of traditional religion and modern science respectively. Technically, they are known as Deontological Ethics and Utilitarian Ethics. There is a third option open to the Jedi – the way of balance.

"Aristotle laid out this way of balance many years ago. His psychology of the soul and its virtues is based on the 'golden mean' or balance between *extremes*. Every ethical virtue is an intermediate

140

condition between *excess* and *deficiency*. Finding this middle ground or 'balance' is essential to reaching well-being, the ultimate form of godlike consciousness. His constant phrase is, '... is the Middle state between ...'

"I'll take a couple of examples from those two negative emotions we talked about before – fear and anger. If I were to ask you what the opposite of fear was, you'd say something like courage or bravery. That gives the impression that there are only two options, two choices, two poles. But is it possible to be too brave, to be so brave that you put your life at risk for no good purpose? For instance, is it brave to throw yourself out of a plane without a parachute, or to face a Sith lord when you are yet an apprentice?

"Aristotle claimed that these are not examples of bravery, but rather recklessness. Remember what Yoda claimed about Luke to Obi-Wan? 'Adventure. Heh! Excitement. Heh! A Jedi craves not these things. You are reckless!' Courage is not an extreme; it is the balanced position between rashness and cowardice. The dark side is all about extremes, in this case a wild negligence or a quivering fear. The Jedi walks between the two.

"Also, there's the case of anger. Imagine if you can, Jedi totally without anger of any sort. What then would motivate such Jedi to right the wrongs they see around them? What would energise them into action? Someone totally without this emotion could have no sense of compassion towards those in distress and need, or no regard for bringing justice to the planet.

"When considering anger, Aristotle saw the way of excess as irascibility, or being easily irritated, and the way of deficiency as 'spiritlessness' or someone who doesn't care about anything. The balance between the two is a moderate temper, or, better, simple patience. Yoda said that the dark side was easy, 'quick to join you in a fight.' Aristotle argreed. Remember his quote?

"'Anyone can become angry - that is easy, but to be angry with the right person at the right time, and for the right purpose and in the right way - that is not within everyone's power and that is not easy.'

"A Jedi Knight strives to achieve balance in life in all their deeds and actions.

"How did Anakin fail to live in this way in his own life?

"Are you 'extreme' in any of your lifestyle choices, either by deficiency or excess?"

As we watch another YouTube vid called 'Golden Mean of Aristotle Part 2' I have a few mean thoughts of my own. Such as.

Balance is boring. That's what my instinct tells me.

It's like saying, *I only want a little bit of pleasure, a little bit of power, a little bit of purpose.* Who would say such a stupid thing?

Yes, I'd like a wife who is fairly beautiful, not a stunner, thank you, but no swamp donkey neither, no sir!

Yes, I'd like a moderate amount of wealth please, enough to keep me from getting my hands on the government handouts I've paid my taxes for, but not enough to live comfortably. Just enough to keep me on the breadline, having to scrimp for each month's mortgage, clothes, electricity and food. Petrol and dignity cost extra.

Yes, I'd like my health to be in between the extremes of *fit-as-a-fiddle* and *I-wish-I-was-dead*. Somewhere around *I'm-off-on-the-sick* would do nicely.

142

This is a philosophy for losers and life-haters if I ever heard one. The stuff about having power over yourself is one thing. I dig that. But this is too far, too *extreme* for me, ha! And life is extreme, extremely fuck-no or extremely fuck-yes. This middle way, it's for the birds.

I'd tell him that too if I didn't think my words would slur.

Maybe a few too many bevies over lunch.

Too many.

Excess.

Oh humph!

Give me a break man.

Chapter 29

Eat the Census Takers

The same generic classroom, Queen's University, Belfast.
Saturday 15 November 2008, 3:09 pm

The break is next, so he promises.

My little recorder is three quarters full so I hope there isn't too much more to go.

My head is clearing now. I'm ready to be stretched.

Just as well.

"Now we come to one of the most difficult concepts for a *padawan* to learn, and one of the hardest mind-skills to learn. It begins with a word that's found scattered throughout the most recent *Star Wars* films. I think that it's the most frequent instruction given to Anakin throughout the course of his life. Yet it's one that he fails most miserably to achieve. I speak about the call to 'mindfulness.'

"When the boy Anakin first stands before the Jedi council and receives a rather harsh round of questions from the council members, Mace Windu tells him to "be mindful" of his feelings. Further on, when Qui-Gon admits to Anakin that he is not allowed to train the boy, he nevertheless instructs young Anakin to watch him carefully and "be mindful" of what he sees. In a later film, after a burst of irritation by Anakin over Padme's seemingly cold reception, Obi Wan criticises him for focusing on the negative and not being "mindful of his thoughts."

"Mindfulness is a big deal in Psychology now. It has different shades of meaning. The most obvious sense is that of self-knowledge. Self-knowledge is the keystone of what we call 'emotional intelligence'. It is the ability to monitor our own feelings, and involves recognising a feeling *as it happens*. These feelings can consist of short-term emotions or longer-term moods. Self-knowledge includes an honest appraisal of your own goals and values. Those strong in this skill can accurately label their own emotions and evaluate their effectiveness from a detached perspective.

"More recently, mindfulness has come into its own as a technique in clinical psychology and psychiatry. In this sphere, mindfulness is a powerful way of reducing stress and dealing with negative thinking. This sort of mindfulness is described as the regular, disciplined practice of moment-to-moment awareness. A mindful person is focused on their present immediate experience. Through practice and discipline, attention is not allowed to wander. Those thoughts and feelings that arise are not judged but accepted; a mindful attitude is open and curious to all things.

"There is much in this that is akin to Buddhist meditative

145

and breathing practices. But there is a third form of mindfulness that is very much orientated in the Western scientific tradition. I will focus on this, not because it is superior, but because I know more about it and it is less widely known to the public than I think it deserves. It is based on the research of Ellen Langer, a professor of Psychology at Harvard University.

"Here's how Langer defines it. 'When we are mindful, we implicitly or explicitly: (1) view a situation from several perspectives, (2) see information presented in the situation as novel, (3) attend to the context in which we are perceiving the information, and eventually (4) create new categories through which this information may be understood.'[10] If that sounds a bit dense, let me sum it up in a sentence – mindfulness is the act of noticing newness in experience. A mindful person will then use this new information as a resource for more accurate and flexible decision-making.

"Still no wiser? Let's run a few of Langer's test programs to check your level of mindfulness and illustrate what it means. There are all taken from her excellent book on *Mindfulness*.

"Test one – Are you mindful of your assumptions, of the way you classify things, of the distinctions you make and how you visualize problems? Acting on an anonymous phone call, the police raid a house to arrest a suspected murderer. They don't know what he looks like but they know his name is John and that he is inside the house. The police burst in on a carpenter, a lorry driver, a mechanic and a fire-fighter all playing poker. Without hesitation or communication of any kind, they immediately arrest the fire-fighter. How do they know they've got their man?

---

[10] Langer,1997, p.111

"Hint: The police only know two things: that the criminal's name is John and that he is in a particular house. Answer: The fire-fighter is the only man in the room. The rest of the poker players are *women*.

"Test two - A man and his son are in a car crash. The father is killed and the child is taken to hospital gravely injured. When he gets there, the surgeon says, 'I can't operate on this boy - for he is my son!' How can this possibly be?

"Hint: This has nothing to do with adoption or time travel. Answer: The surgeon cannot operate on her own son; *she* is his *mother*.

"Test three - How many 'F's are there in this sentence (reading it only once)? **"FINAL FOLIOS SEEM TO RESULT FROM YEARS OF DUTIFUL STUDY OF TEXTS ALONG WITH YEARS OF SCIENTIFIC EXPERIENCE"**

"The answer is eight.

"Test four – Q: What do we call a tree that grows from acorns? A: Oak. What do we call a funny story? A: Joke. Q: What do we call the sound made by a frog? A: Croak. Q: What do we call the white of an egg? A: Yolk. Wrong – we call it 'the white.'

"Test five – Around 2 a.m. your door rings. Outside is an expensively dressed man in a Ferrari. He apologises and explains that he is in a scavenger hunt he is desperate to win. One of the objects he needs is a piece of wood 3 by 7 feet. If you can help him, he'll give you £50,000. You believe him, but you have no wood in your garage, you know none of your friends and neighbours will have any, and all the shops are closed. What do you do?

147

"Hint: Really see what's in front of you! Answer: Give him your door.

"These are more than mere puzzles. They test a certain mindset, a mindset that every Jedi strives strive to obtain. It is characterised by curiosity and a desire to investigate. A mindful person is open to new ways of doing things, and able to produce insights that are innovative. They have the ability to behave in different ways according to the situation. They notice what people are up to. They see the big picture and not just the immediate facts. They are open-mind about everything, even things that challenge their core beliefs.

"This is very different from a Sith attitude, which we might characterize as *mindless*. Sith work from traditional categories, otherwise known as stereotypes and 'isms'. Their thinking and behaviour is automatic, instinctive, without reflection or self-assessment. They view reality from single perspectives, with no ability or desire to alter their 'point of view' or empathise with another being. They work from unexamined assumptions. They focus on the outcome they want to achieve, not caring about the process that leads to it.

"The development of mindfulness is an essential skill for a Jedi to master. But it is also one of the most difficult skills, requiring much in the way of thought and reflection. You must begin to grow the skill of 'thinking about your thinking.' Do you know how you view the world? How you judge others? Why you react the way you do?

"If you're still confused, watch this YouTube video called 'Mindfulness - An Introduction' by PositivePsychology and see that it helps."

All this is quite new to me so I need to tread with caution.

Nevertheless, my first cogitation is, *What a fecken nerve*!

If I've understood him right, he's making Jedi the broad-minded, Western liberal types, while the Sith are reduced to some sort of judgmental fundamentalists!

Well allow me to retort.

"I've a question for you."

"Go ahead."

"So you're saying that Jedi are the real relativists while the Sith are absolutists. Is that so?"

"Yes," he says, and waits.

"But the Jedi are the ones that believe in an absolute distinction between the light side and the dark side. They classify the dark side as evil. Surely the Sith are the relativists, the pragmatists, since they use whatever works. They don't care about ethics. Only results."

Now all the class perks up their ears.

"Excellent point. The Force is strong in this one!"

Everyone laughs. Minus one.

"Does anyone have an answer for the Sith in the front row?"

No-one speaks. Then him.

"OK. I'll have a go then. I'd make two points, or a point and a question. There's a difference between believing that everything is relative and believing that everything is from a perspective or point of view. I'd argue that the Jedi hold to the latter, not the former. They believe in a total distinction between the light side and the dark side. That's why they expel Jedi who to any degree dabble with the dark. But also, here's your question. You think that the Sith don't hold to any absolutes. What about power? Isn't that their absolute? Isn't power their goal, their method, their code, their reason for existence? Power, absolute power, for its own sake?"

At least I think this is what he says. I can't really remember. I sit their nodding my head as if drawing in his sage words. All I can recall is what he said at the start, what he said about me, the classification he set upon me.

The Sith in the front row.

Is that who I am?

Is that what I am to be?

This is the question that digs deep into my mind as we spill out for our final break.

Chapter 30

Monsters from the Id

The same generic classroom, Queen's University, Belfast.
Saturday 15 November 2008, 3:44 pm

My mind brims over with questions I cannot answer. Yet.

Such as: What's the real difference between a Jedi and a Sith?

Such as: If there's a course of Jedi training, is there one for Sith too?

Such as: Why would someone become a Sith? What's the motivation here? (OK that's two questions.)

Such as: Is *this* my destiny?

Such as: How am I going to make six cigarettes last me the rest of the day?

Important questions like that.

He starts again.

"How did Anakin fall from grace?

"Finally, we've come to the missing skill which led to Anakin's ultimate downfall – detachment. Anakin's *Achilles' heel* was his attachment to Padme and his fear of losing her as he lost his mother. He acknowledges the Jedi doctrine to her in plain language. 'Attachment is forbidden. Possession is forbidden.' Obi-Wan admits his misgivings about Anakin to Mace Windu. 'He has a... an emotional connection with her. It's been there since he was boy. Now he's confused...distracted.'

"In my opinion, it is possible to trace the exact point at which Anakin ceased to be a Jedi. It occurs during a very telling discussion with Yoda in which he tells of his visions of suffering and death. Yoda tells Anakin to let go. 'Attachment leads to jealousy. The shadow of greed, that is.'

This is exactly the trajectory that Anakin's life will now take. Yoda senses this and gives Anakin his final orders, the advice he needs if he is to remain a Jedi and complete his training. 'Train yourself to let go of everything you fear to lose.' Anakin chooses another way.

"It reminds me of a quote from the film *Heat* with Robert De Niro and Al Pachino. 'A guy told me one time, don't let yourself get attached to anything you are not willing to walk out on in 30 seconds flat if you feel the heat around the corner. That's the discipline.'

"All very well for a cool movie line, but can there be any substance to it? Actually, yes, and we can take our cue from another movie – Gladiator. Do you remember the name of the old emperor played by Richard Harris? His name was Marcus Aurelius and he belonged to a school of Philosophy called Stoicism.

152

Stoicism is I think the closest the West has to offer to a discipline of detachment.

"What is Stoicism? Stoicism was a school of Hellenistic philosophy, founded in Athens by Zeno of Citium in the early third century BC. Stoicism taught the development of self-control and fortitude as a means of overcoming destructive emotions. It became the foremost popular philosophy among the educated elite in the Graeco-Roman Empire and hence helped produce what we call 'the West.'

"Stoic ethics taught freedom from passion as the key to well-being, virtue and peace of mind. The ancient meaning of *passion* was 'anguish' or 'suffering,' that is, 'passively' reacting to external events. Their goal was to be free of suffering through *apathy* — being objective or eradicating the emotional response to external events (the things we cannot control). They trained their attention to remain in the present moment (similar to some forms of Eastern meditation).

"Here are some good quotes from a Stoic philosopher and former slave called Epictetus. 'Freedom is secured not by the fulfilling of one's desires, but by the removal of desire.' 'Permit nothing to cleave to you that is not your own; nothing to grow to you that may give you agony when it is torn away.' And the classic – 'Man is disturbed not by things, but by the views he takes of them.'

"Stoicism is the closest thing I know to a real-life Jedi philosophy. A mature Jedi Knight should develop a deliberate sense of apathy and indifference towards things that are irrelevant to his or her mission in life. Make a list of things that you should not care about and need to detach yourself from. Then think about

153

how you are going to do it."

It can't be as simple as that. *Anakin became Sith over a girl?* That's the stupidest thing I've heard since Gerry Spice became a UN Ambassador. What, did Padme lure him to the dark side with her little black number? Doesn't make sense; she wasn't even a Sith! There must be more to it. Think!

What did Anakin fear? Loosing Padme as he lost his mother? That's what our Jedi teacher said. Anakin would not detach from them. He wanted her to live like he wanted his mother to live. He did not even want death to part them. He loved life. He wanted to overcome death. He wanted his love to last forever. Immortality.

Alright, let's flip it over. If the Sith goal is to escape the separation of death, then what is the Jedi aim? Detachment. To detach from death! To separate themselves from the fear of death, and anger at death's separations. Freedom from the desire to live!

If the Jedi way is one of detachment from life, the Sith way is one of involvement in life and enthusiasm over all that life has to offer! Interest in life's affairs. Participation in life pleasures and pains. Association with other beings. Concern for their flourishing! Loving life so much that they strive for it never to end! Is this the dark side, wanting to overcome death? And is the light side nothing more than a hatred for life?

Just when I'm about to run out of exclamation marks and question marks, group work intervenes. I've been so much in the 'flow' of thinking just then that I didn't notice the YouTube video called 'History of Stoicism Documentary' are the scraggy circle of chairs forming around me.

The Dutch guy speaks.

154

"Hey, that was a pretty decent film clip I thought. So we have to make some sort of list together, right? Stuff we could detach ourselves from, or from which we should detach ourselves, should I say? Seems kind of a personal thing to me though, 'cause like, everyone's would be different, I think."

What I think is, *No they wouldn't, you stuud. Everyone here will form the same humdrum, self-righteous list. We should detach from what people think about us. We should detach from materialistic concerns and status symbols. We should detach from our addictions, our obsessions. We should detach from a belief that we can rescue other adults. I can see it all coming with a deathly sense of inevitability. PS Spare some weed?*

"OK," I say. "I'll play scribe again. Let's go round in a circle and make one contribution each. Let's try to keep it specific, name actual items or events or situations we'd like to detach. I'll start. Religious sensitivities."

"What? What was that?" says a chubby twenty-something, charity-shop victim beside me. I think it's female.

"Religious sensitivities. The need to believe. The god-shaped hole. Conscience and guilt. All that. I'd like myself deprogrammed. Detached."

"Oh. I feel dumb now. I was going to say something a bit less grand? (Titters) I've got this chocolate doughnut fixation? (Titters) I kind of love them and hate them? (Titters) So that's mine."

"So which do you want to detach from?" I ask. "The love or the hate? Just so I know what to write down."

At first she looks at me as if I'm the stupid one. Does that count as irony in the strict, classical sense?

155

"The love, duh! So then I wouldn't have to eat them anymore."

There are no titters now.

"Why would you want to detach from something you love?" I say. "Wouldn't it be better to detach from the hate so you could enjoy them in peace?"

"But they're bad for me."

I spy tears. But I've detached myself from sympathy.

But they're bad for me. Like the doughnuts do it, make her eat them, send telepathic messages to her *id* saying 'Eat us, eat us, we are the manna of life'. No, Fat One, that's not how it works. Take responsibility. You chose to eat each and every doughnut. You are not forced. You are not coerced. You cause it to happen. You will it. Then you whine about the outcome. Here's the iron law of the universe - You cannot detach choice from consequences, not even if you become a Jedi Knight.

I look to the person next to her with expectation, pen at the ready, and ignore the dark glares emanating from the others. You might say I've detached myself from them. This detachment thing is great. I'm a natural at it. When it suits me. No principle above myself.

This time I've got a little, mouse-like girl, not bad looking in Northern Ireland terms, which is to say, about a three-and-a-half out of ten. Actually, she's quite tall for a girl, with dull, blond highlights, but she's having trouble dragging her eyes from her knees right now. I don't recollect hearing her voice throughout the whole day so far. I'm going to change that.

"So. What's your contribution?"

She literally doesn't move. She could teach classes to the

Red Injuns – or Native Americans, or whatever they call themselves in our post *Dances With Wolves* universe – on How To Remain Still. I break off the rubber from the end of my pencil and throw it at her face for a reaction. No I don't. But I'd love to do things like that. Just do them. Stuff the consequences. Stuff the conventions. Stuff common sense and anything else starting with 'c.'

"I'd like to. Detach. Myself. From what. People. Think."

It's a miracle, the Silent One awakes! And then spoils it by saying something completely the same.

I look at her in her dismal, self-imposed shyness and think, *What you need, love, is a good dose of Sith training. You don't need more serenity, you've already got it coming out of every pore. You need to learn how to kick ass and take names, how to live fast and die young, and other similar clichés! You need your world shaken up, not down. You need to learn how to use obscene language, damnable lies, psychological manipulation, social power plays, and sexual allure. You need to become your own fucking goddess, literally. But you won't find such teaching here. And if not here, then where? Where?*

'Here' is about to disappear into nothingness with the final session of today.

Chapter 31

Campbell's Preserve

The same generic classroom, Queen's University, Belfast.
Saturday 15 November 2008, 4:24 pm

True story.

Now when I was a young boy, at the age of five, my mum believed I was gonna be, the greatest priest alive. But now I'm a man, a little past thirty one, I want you to believe me, baby, I've had way too much, of what passes for fun.

Ain't that a Sith?

She realised I was unlikely to transform into priest material when the bed-wetting, fire-starting and pet-provoking behaviour manifested itself from an early age. But there's still a little bit of the priest in me. Poverty, I know. It's all about giving money away as quickly as I get my hands on it. Chastity? I've been celibate in my heart life-long, with one minor lapse. Obedience? Well, I don't obey anybody, if that counts, even myself. Which means I obey everything, every whim and tickle that nature sends my way. The power and the glory of it all.

I'm thinking of *priests* because Baird reminds me of a *minister* ascending his pulpit, a modern day Father Mapple all ready to buoy us up and cast us off. He thinks, beyond these walls, there be monsters. Well maybe there are monsters within them too.

He starts his last homily.

"By this time, you've heard most of what I have to say. I've given you a little Jedi background. I've tested your sensitivity to the Force. I've told you what skills you need to build up, and I've pointed out what can bring you down. Now it's over to you. The journey is yours alone.

"Or is it? This is where things get a rather interesting, not to say philosophical. There's much *in Star Wars* about destiny. And then there's much about choice. Here we find in modern pop-culture the tip of an ago-old debate about determinism and free-will. Which is right? Was Luke destined to defeat, or convert, Vader and restore balance to the Force? If so, did he have a choice, or was he carried along, automatically, by the will of the Force? But if he did have a choice, how could there be a prophecy? Or a universe of balance? Or a definite 'happy ending?'

"Could Luke have become a Sith? Or a failed Jedi? Or remained a farmboy?

"We've seen already that Luke's path was a difficult one. Although, from one perspective, *Star Wars* is a kid's movie, yet, like I said, there was a lot of hard stuff for him to deal with. Sometimes he chose against the advice of his mentors. Sometimes it seemed he would give way to anger and revenge. It was no easy

159

ride. But was it free? Yes, he chose, but he also seemed to be borne along by the wings of destiny.

"To solve this puzzle, and find direction for ourselves, we need to look at something I've already mentioned – the hero's journey. The main protagonist in a story passes through from beginning to end according to a *universal pattern*. Every story doesn't have every part of the journey. But those who've studied ancient myths have gathered together their findings into one pattern, one cycle. There are different versions but the one I'm showing you today was formalised by a guy called Joseph Campbell. He is doubly significant for us because George Lucas claims Campbell was a big influence on his *Star Wars* plot. Although Campbell focused on ancient myths, you can see his pattern at work in characters from Neo to Harry Potter to Frodo.

"First, there's *the call to adventure*. Princess Leia sends a plea for help to Jedi Knight Obi-Wan (Ben) Kenobi on the planet of Tatooine. Destiny, in the form of Jawa traders, brings her message to Luke Skywalker, a young farm boy. When Luke sees the message hologram, he is drawn into a quest to rescue the Princess and ultimately to save the galaxy.

"Luke is initially reticent – *the refusal of the call*. He has his aunt and uncle to think of, and his farm duties to attend to. They have already forbidden him from attending the academy and joining the rebellion. But, when the Empire destroys his family, they unwitting release Luke from the call to an ordinary life and set him on his way.

"Often the inexperienced hero finds that he cannot proceed without help or *supernatural aid*. And often this takes the form of a wise guide who provides advice and equipment to advance the quest. Ben fills this role and donates a special token - a lightsaber that once belonged to Luke's father. Luke's mentor also interprets the Princess' message and introduces Luke to the spiritual power known as 'the Force.'

"The hero must discard his familiar life for a journey of transformation from childhood to adulthood. Luke *crosses the first threshold* of his journey at Mos Eisley spaceport. Here he encounters danger, but he also finds a hero-partner in the form of Han Solo, a pirate and smuggler. Ben begins to train Luke in the ways of the Force.

"As the heroes approach Alderaan, they find that the planet has been destroyed by the Death Star, a colossal giant Imperial space station. The Death Star is a technological labyrinth; a maze of hallways, passages, dead ends, and bottomless trenches. Campbell calls this *the belly of the whale*. Like traditional knights, Han Solo and Luke wear armour to accomplish their first hero deed - the Princess rescue.

"Next, Princess Leia leads Han Solo and Luke to the Rebel base to plan an attack on the Death Star. Luke joins the Rebellion. Uniformed and ready, his youthful identity fades, replaced by that of a heroic pilot, ready to sacrifice his life for a cause.

"In the end, good triumphs over evil, and the heroes are recognised for their deeds of valour. This moment is the end of one adventure, but it also represents the start of the next. Luke has been *initiated* into herohood.

"Midway through the hero's journey, he traverses a perilous *road of trials* that uncovers crucial moments of self-knowledge. Although the Death Star has been destroyed, the powers of darkness have not been conquered. The Empire has pursued the Rebels to

161

the ice planet of Hoth, where the heroes, facing new dangers from predatory creatures and the harsh climate, and are forced to flee during an Imperial attack.

"The *sacred grove* is another mythic motif; it represents an enclosure where the hero is transformed. When Luke leaves Hoth, he travels to the planet Dagobah to undergo training with the Jedi Master, Yoda. Forests can symbolise magic and the unconscious mind, where there are secrets to be discovered. In this forest Luke battles an image of Vader, foreshadowing his combat with the Dark Lord later in the story.

"At this difficult and dangerous juncture on the hero path, Han Solo and Luke reaffirm the meaning and value of their lives by demonstrating their willingness to *sacrifice* themselves. The danger of illusion is symbolised by Cloud City above the planet Bespin. At first the city appears transcendent as it floats among the clouds, but it has a dark underside that becomes a crucible of pain and betrayal for the heroes. Luke is lured while Han Solo is captured.

"The hero's journey sometimes includes a *father quest*. After many ordeals, the hero finds his father and unites with him. This is known as *atonement with the father*. Luke has tried to follow in his father's footsteps as a heroic pilot and Jedi Knight. The dark, unknown side of his father - and of himself - is now unveiled as Luke confronts Vader in the dark passage of Cloud City.

"Vader reveals to Luke that he is his father. As Luke acknowledges him they begin to move toward reconciliation. Luke has recognised the dark side of himself as part of his destiny, and Darth Vader has begun his own journey toward transformation. This is the *ultimate boon* or gift that Luke received: a knowledge of who he is and what will also prove to be the Empire's undoing.

"The *hero's return* marks the end of Luke's trials. The hero must return from his adventures with the means to benefit his society. As the story continues, all the characters undergo changes: Han Solo is resurrected from his carbonite tomb; Lando atones for his betrayal of Han Solo by assisting in his rescue, and Princess Leia assures the end of Jabba's reign of tyranny by destroying him.

"While the Rebels continue to struggle against Imperial tyranny, the Empire is constructing a new Death Star. Luke discovers that Princess Leia, who has guided and supported him throughout his journey, is his twin sister. He also finds that he must confront his father again. Yet when they make mind-to-mind contact through the Force, Darth Vader appears uncertain rather than aggressive - a sign that he is beginning a transformation.

"The inhabitants of an *enchanted forest* can be both dangerous and helpful. The hero must be aware of right magic to use to evoke their protective powers. Luke secures the help of the Ewoks, the small furry inhabitants of the forest moon of Endor. Their lush green environment and harmony with nature make a obviously warm contrast to the austere technology of the Empire.

"Meanwhile, Luke realizes that he must take a different route from his friends to attempt to reach that part of Darth Vader that is still his father and to turn him back from the dark side.

"The heroes must at the last enter *the heart of darkness*, the fortress of Evil itself, to destroy its stronghold. When Han Solo and Princess Leia finally destroy the energy shield generator, Lando and Wedge fly into the Death Star to fire on the reactor core at the centre of the space station. While conflict rages around the Death Star, Luke struggles with the dark forces within the Death Star, where he is undergoing a spiritual conflict in his battle of wills with the Emperor.

"In his confrontation with Darth Vader and the Emperor, Luke gains *final victory* not by his warrior skills, but with an appeal to his father's heart. It is Darth Vader who slays the Emperor to save his son. At the climax of the *Star Wars* trilogy, he even asks Luke to unmask him. The dropping of the mask visually represents Darth Vader's release from the imprisonment of his role, unfortunately for him, only at the moment of death. Yet this gesture is also an affirmation of life, the final opening up of father to son.

"As the Rebels and Ewoks celebrate the destruction of the Death Star and their victory over the Empire, Luke burns his father's armour on a funeral pyre. The spirit of Luke's father, Anakin Skywalker, joins the spirits of Ben and Yoda. Luke has achieved the final triumph of the mythic hero's journey. He has brought back from his adventures the means for the regeneration of his society. He has reached *journey's end*.

"This is the map. But the map is not the territory, as Alfred Korzybski put it. You have to search out the reality for yourself. What destiny will you chose?"

Speaking as an anthropologist (don't laugh) I find this familiar. I can detect the scent of Arnold van Gennep and Victor Turner a block away. The old knowledge comes flooding back. Might I find a use for it, after all? A minor miracle surely!

I feel I have drunk Baird dry so I leave immediately. Many of his sycophants seem to want to linger and lick his arse. No thanks. I have a delicate palate when it comes to osculation.

And even more delicate when it comes to choosing destinies. Isn't that a paradox? If it's a destiny, already determined, how can you choose it? Tell the truth, I don't care. I'll leave the metaphysics for priests. As a young man, I asked a Jesuit if they still taught that the end justified the means. He replied, shifting from one foot to the other, that, 'We don't do that anymore.' I was devastated. Since they value their ends so little themselves, it was the end of it all for me.

I've now stepped outside the ridiculously named Peter Froggatt Centre. The early evening is clear and fresh. So I make straightway for the darkest, dingiest pub available. Since this is the heart of Belfast's student land, the search takes me approximately three minutes. A number of perfection, indeed.

I once saw an episode of Rebus in which he listed his two primary skills as drinking and thinking, preferably at the same time A man after my own heart, minus the sentiment, stomach and other Scottish stereotypes.

Now to the real choice. Does my heroic destiny tonight lie with Glenfiddich or J&B?

Chapter 32

Ouroboros Eats

Place: Northern Ireland
Time: Later that night...
Setting: Their different houses
Viewpoint: First Allen, them Mark

Allen

Before the day started I was enervated. Now I'm totally tired and shagged out after a long squawk. A day of intense training like that always wastes my batteries, especially if it's over the weekend. It was a high effort workshop.

I didn't eat lunch because a journalist from Dublin wanted an interview. But who can bellyache at free publicity?

The students scored eight and a half out of ten, all forty or so of them. They took a while to warm up but once they got going, there were plenty of intelligent questions and debate. I enjoy that.

And an unexpected demographic mix too. Maybe half in half gender wise, which is a first. Even some older people who'd never seen the films. Hard to fathom, but fair play anyway.

Excellent evaluations from them all about the workshop. I glanced over the sheets as I tidied the room at the end. Students were lining up to talk with me afterwards. A few want to meet me to talk about other work related projects, public and health sectors. That's an encouraging sign too after all the time I've pumped in to this.

I earned me a round of applause at the end which took me by surprise. Perhaps it shows manners more than satisfaction. Maybe I'm too hard on myself like my wife says. Unless every student has a life-changing experience during the day, I'm not satisfied. Which is to say, I'm never satisfied.

That's not strictly true; one guy said my work had altered his life, that argumentative bloke at the front. I was too taken aback to tell if he was joking or not, then, and I'm too tired now. I wanted to speak some more with that guy. I would have succeeded if it wasn't for those pesky fire alarms.

What did it achieve? Anything?

That's the end of it.

Mark

My hands are shaking now. Quivering with life. Or the water of life. The effect is the same.

I stayed to the end.

He fixed it so I actually stayed to the end.

I didn't expect to go never mind stay to the end.

You can tell my excitement at having stayed to the end.

167

That's why I keep repeating it and repeating it and repeating it.

The end. End. Not in the sense of termination but as in goal, target, *telos*.

I haven't stayed to the end of anything much recently except the dregs of a bottle. That must *mean* something.

What?

I don't know but I'll find out. It's time to hit the internet. I've some research to do. No. No. That's not right. I've got a fucking *journey* going on here. A beginning. A first step.

A new start.

A New Hope.

Chapter 33

Beware of Your Dreams

Blog by Allen on 21 November 2008.

The UK's First University Jedi Course

Last Saturday (15th November) I delivered my long-anticipated university workshop on *Star Wars* called *Feel the Force: How to Train in the Jedi Way*. There was an excellent turn-out (over 30 apprentices from all ages, genders and species) with fabulous feedback. We had a great time together; lots of humour, lots of discussion, plenty of new ideas to ponder, students left hungry for more. All a training session should be.

Five interesting things came out of it:
(1) People from different employment sectors enquired if I could provide business training for them based on the workshop. Some wanted the *Star Wars* link, others were keen on the fact that I made

standard training topics - Assertiveness, Emotional Intelligence, Ethics - interesting. I didn't foresee this (so maybe I'm not much of a Jedi), but it's an exciting development. I'm due to give a couple of Jedi-themed corporate talks in December for the Institute of Internal Auditors (in Belfast and Dublin). May the Force be with them!

(2) There was a contingent of journalists there, so the story still has resonance with the public-at-large. May the Force be with them too!

(3) No-one turned up in *Star Wars* costumes, so it wasn't just a geek-fest (although a few of the guys did know a scary amount about *Star Wars*). One guy wore a tee-shirt of Yoda as a police mug-shot, but that was cool, not nerdy.

(4) The whole thing was recorded for a *Star Wars* docu-film that's coming out soon - learn about it here.

(5) Such was the response that I've decided to propose another workshop in Queen's for the Spring Term. There were so many topics I could have included but didn't due to lack of time. So get ready for round two. I'll tell you more about it soon.

It's been a great adventure, designing and delivering this workshop. Join in it with me. Let me know your thoughts.

Chapter 34

Go With Him Twain

Outlined below is a copy of Allen's second course proposal to Queen's University Belfast, following his massively successful first Jedi workshop.
Sent - Tuesday 25 Nov 2008.

COURSE PROPOSAL

Course Title

Please supply a short title that we can use in our brochure:
The Force Strikes Back: How to Train in the Jedi Way

Course Description

Please supply a description (maximum 60 words) for inclusion in our brochure. Open Learning reserves the right to edit course descriptions:

Last year saw the UK's first Jedi university course here at QUB.

Due to international media interest and inspiring feedback from participants, this workshop is back, with new topics! Learn the Jedi arts of negotiation and conflict resolution. Increase your agility and enhance your senses. Read the minds of others. Learn to use your intuition. Participation in the first workshop is not necessary to enjoy this one.

Chapter 35

Octavio Ocampo

Blog by Allen on 26 November 2008.

Jedi Knights – Myth and Reality

Once the publicity for the Jedi workshop started to skyrocket (or is it skywalk?) I was repeatedly asked a particular question. Even if it wasn't asked explicitly, I could see it in people's smirking eyes, and feel it in the draught from their open mouths.

"You don't think all this Jedi stuff is *really real*, do you?"

It's not as silly a question as it first sounds. After all, there are people out there who take this Jedi thing very seriously. Some have built the beginnings of a religion around it. Others talk earnestly of trying to live out 'the Jedi way' and of their temptations toward 'the dark side'.

I had two standard responses, both of which I think are still pretty much on target. The first was, no, I don't think the Jedi are real. I'm only using *Star Wars* as *a platform from which to launch a learning experience* involving things that are real - skills in communication, concentration and control. I'm trying to make it interesting, that's all.

The second was related to it. Do the Scouts have to believe that the works of Rudyard Kipling are literally true in order to profit from Kim's Game or accept Akela as a model mentor figure? I'm still thinking of answers to this question, and here's are some arguments I've come up with. Tell me what you think.

(1) Philosophically, there is no such thing as the 'really real'. All viewing of reality is 'seeing-as' (as, for example, with Jastrow's duck-rabbit, made famous by Wittgenstein). The *meaning* of reality is the *use* we put it to, what we do with it, how we choose to apply it in our lives. (Again, thank Wittgenstein, the greatest philosopher of the 20th century, for this insight.) All our knowledge of the world has a personal element; this includes even scientific descriptions of the world, which are supposed to represent the pinnacle of objectivity. (Thomas Kuhn, the great philosopher of science, again used the duck-rabbit to illustrate his notion of a 'paradigm shift' or the sociological/subjective element in scientific advancement.) 'Nuff said!

(2) Do characters have to be historical for us to regard them as role models or inspirational heroes? Alexander the Great modeled himself on Homer's Achilles, while Teddy Roosevelt took

174

inspiration from a character in one of Marryat's books. Many detectives draw stimulation from Sherlock Holmes, while leaders look to Shakespeare's Henry the Fifth. As Martin Seligman says in his classic book, *Authentic Happiness* (138), "Role models and paragons in the culture compellingly illustrate a strength or virtue. Models may be real (Mahatma Gandhi and humane leadership), apocryphal (George Washington and honesty), or explicitly mythic **(Luke Skywalker and flow)**." The bold is mine!

(3) There's something about the ideal of a warrior-monk - which is essentially what the Jedi are - that strikes deep into our subconscious. There have been many historic examples of warrior-monks in both East and West. Believe it or not, there were plans in the 60s to form a New Age kind of warrior-monk for the US Army (known as the First Earth Battalion). There was also an alleged attempt to create a super-soldier by the US in the 70s. The name of the venture? Project Jedi. On the internet you can easily find interesting attempts to base life coaching on the ideal.

So what I'm basically saying is (1) the Jedi can be 'real' in some sense (2) even though they are fictional characters (3) because of their psychological impact and mythological resonance.

So get over it.

Chapter 36

Battlefield Work

Presentation delivered to the Irish Institute of Internal Auditors.
Belfast – 9 December 2008
Dublin – 10 December 2008

PowerPoint (PPT) 1
[Title slide]
Star Wars Goes To Work; or How to use Jedi mind-tricks in your job to get your way, become indispensable, and stay sane
by Allen Baird PhD JGM

PPT 2
[Photos of my university Jedi event]
A long time ago, in a university far, far, away... Showing at a media outlet near you!

PPT 3

How weird is all this?

So I looked up the definition of 'auditors'...

"Auditing was developed by L. Ron Hubbard, and is described by the Church of Scientology as 'spiritual counseling which is the central practice of Dianetics and Scientology'"!

PPT 3

A quick geek check!

Who here has:

- Watched the films
- Collected the models
- Read the novels
- Gone to a convention
- Dressed up in the costumes

PPT 4

How many have NEVER seen a *Star Wars* film?

PPT 5

A summary of the plot of *Star Wars* (according to a 3 year-old)

PPT 6

This afternoon's agenda...

How to use Jedi mind-tricks at work to:

1. Get your own way
2. Become indispensible
3. Stay sane

[Each of these three sections is underlines below.]

PPT 7

How to get your way

PPT 8

Mind-trick # 1 – Influence the weak minded!

PPT 9

Behold – the Jedi mind-trick!

PPT 10

***Who* do you need to influence?**

- Your boss – Jabba
- Your clients – the clones
- Your colleagues – Han & Leia

PPT 11

The quickest way to influence others – assertiveness (compared with passive, aggressive and passive-aggressive)

PPT 12

How assertive are you?

- Passive – C3PO
- Aggressive – Darth Vader
- Passive-Aggressive – the Emperor
- Assertive – Princess Leia

PPT 13

The assertiveness test

1. If a colleague asks you to do something that isn't in your remit, what would you do?

(a) Try to fit it in – it's nice to be helpful.

(b) Do it if you want to but use it as a way to learn and built up trust.

(c) Refuse totally – it's their problem, not yours, what are you, a charity?

PPT 14

2. How do you feel about your managers?

(a) I worry that they don't think much of me.

(b) I respect their experience and feel that we're all part of the same team.

(c) I think they're a bunch of wasters, so I try to avoid them so I can get on with my job in peace.

PPT 15

3. How often do you feel 'put upon' at work?

(a) Regularly, but it is what I expect.

(b) I generally feel in control of my workload.

(c) Colleagues have finally realised that I am not to be imposed upon and know to keep their distance.

PPT 16

4. How do you feel when your opinion is asked?

(a) I am flattered as it happens so rarely.

(b) I feel satisfied that they value my judgments.

(c) They all know my opinions already – if they have to ask they weren't listening!

PPT 17

'Jedi' Assertiveness Techniques

- Use of a power word ('I' & 'No')
- Stating of request or need
- 'Broken record' technique
- Use of consequences
- Body language

[Each of these is illustrated from the films.]

PPT 18

Assertive body language...NOT!

PPT 19

Assertive body language

- Eye contact - good contact without staring
- Facial expression - interested, steady, relaxed
- Movements and gestures – open, tilted
- Positioning – appropriate distance, pointed
- Stance and posture – upright, still, spacious
- Voice – clear, firm, congruous

PPT 20

The four ways to influence others

- Empathising – Clinton
- Energising – Obama
- Arguing – Brown
- Asserting – Thatcher

PPT 21

How *not* to smile... Gordon Brown

PPT 22

How *not* to dress... Billery

PPT 23

Mind-trick # 2 – I can sense your presence!

PPT 24

What is the main social skill?

- Maniac conversation – Mrs Doyle
- Unthreatening charm – Daniel O'Donnell
- Witty repartee – Dylan Moran
- Sexy charisma – George Best

PPT 25

Empathy – The Prime Social Skill

- Telepathy - "I sense your feelings without you expressing them to me in any normal way."
- Sympathy – "I'm sense your sadness, and wish to help."
- Emotional Contagion – "I feel like this because you do."
- Apathy – "I don't give a rat's a%*?e how you feel."
- Empathy – "I sense your sadness."

PPT 26

But how does it work?

- ➢ "Just as the mode of the rational mind is words, the mode of the emotions is nonverbal." (Daniel Goleman)
- ➢ The key to sensing other people's emotions lies in the ability to read **non-verbal cues** – voice tone, gesture, facial expressions, posture, silence (*how* not *what* we say)

181

PPT 27

Elements of Non-Verbal Communication (NVC) and 55/38/7 rule

PPT 28

Power of NVC

- What you can't do [read minds']
- What you shouldn't do [manipulate]
- What you can do
    - Recognise their emotions
    - Simulate the external behaviour associated with it ('motor mimicry')
    - Reciprocate the feeling in yourself due to the stimulation of your own emotional memory
    - Communicate this understanding to the other person in appropriate behaviour

PPT 29

Mirror, Mirror...

[I give an explanation of the mirror phenomenon and technique in psychology.]

PPT 30

E-directed thinking and eye test

[I describe the work of Simon Baron-Cohen on devising tests to measure empathy levels by the ability to decode facial expressions.]

PPT 31

How to become indispensable

PPT 32

Mind-trick # 3 – Use your instincts!

PPT 33

The latest cutting-edge research on the human brain

PPT 34

Left and Right brain functions

[I provide a brief description of brain lateralisation.]

PPT 35

Henry Ford and Fredrick Taylor vs. Malcolm McDowell and Gary Klein

[This represents an emphasis on scientific decision-making in opposition to the place of instinct.]

PPT 36

A New Hope – Daniel Pink and his six senses

[I offer book plug on *A Whole New Mind: Why Right-Brainers Will Rule the Future*.]

PPT 37

Mind-trick # 4 – Feel the flow!

PPT 38

I haven't just made this up, you know! – Martin Seligman in *Authentic Happiness*

[On page Seligman provides Luke Skywalker as an exemplar in the mastery of the mental state of 'flow'.]

PPT 39

A question for you... What is your favourite activity in the world?

PPT 40

Have you ever felt like this when performing some favourite activity?

- You feel completely 'at one' with what you are doing so that you become your verb
- You know you are strong and able to control your destiny... at least for the moment
- You gain an immediate sense of pleasure independent of longer term results or goals
- You lose track of time because you're engrossed

PPT 41

What is this 'flow'?

PPT 42

Why is it called 'flow'?

PPT 43

Between ability and challenge there is the flow...

PPT 44

Another book plug!

[This time I encourage the audience to read a copy of *Flow: The Psychology of Optimum Experience* by Mihaly Csikszentmihalyi.]

PPT 45

How to stay sane

PPT 46

Mind-trick # 5 – Beware of the dark side!

PPT 47

Me and my shadow...

- The shadow is part of the unconscious mind that is the most primitive and irrational
- Jung called it "a reservoir for human darkness"
- Others call it *the dark side of human nature*

PPT 48

The path to the dark side of work

[The reality of anger and depression in the workplace is real and prevalent.]

PPT 49

The link between anger and fear

PPT 50

How to be brave

[I suggest different techniques for increasing person resilience and confidence i.e. the virtue of 'courage'.]

PPT 51

Fake it until you make it!

[An explanation of how our bodily behaviour can affect our emotional state.]

PPT 52

Wise words from an ancient Master – Aristotle on anger

PPT 53

Allen's personal anger management toolkit

1. I challenge my attitude towards how I view anger i.e. see it as immature, bestial, easy
2. I learn to express my feelings appropriately and skilfully i.e. by *assertive* communication
3. I find constructive channels for my anger energy, or a positive cause to put it to
4. I get the &$£% out of there before I put my fist through something for fun... really!

PPT 54

Mind-trick # 6 – Be mindful of your thoughts!

PPT 55

Misunderstood Optimism - What kind of things do you think of when someone is described as an 'optimistic' person? Here's what I (naturally) think...

[I show pollyannaish pictures of fluffy rabbits, love hearts and other sentimental symbols.]

PPT 56

Powerful Optimism

Research shows that...

1. Cultivation of an optimistic mindset significantly increases your chances of health, wealth, and happiness.
2. Success results not only from talent and drive but also optimism.

PPT 57

Real Optimism

Optimism is properly defined in terms of *how you explain to yourself* your own successes and failures ('explanatory style') to equip you to cope with trouble.

- **Optimist** – failure this time is due to something than can be changed
- **Pessimists** – failure due to a lasting characteristic that they are helpless to change

PPT 58

'Explanatory styles' – how optimists and pessimists think

PPT 59

For example, let's say that you've failed your Institute for Internal Auditors exam (for the 13th time...)

[I give examples of how to 'reframe' seeming failures so as to de-catastrophise and learn from them.]

PPT 60

Mind-trick # 7 – Let it go!

PPT 61

What happens when you let it go – Luke destroys the Death Star

PPT 62

What happens when you don't let it go – Anakin becomes Sith

PPT 63

At the movies – James Bond, Heat and Gladiator

[I give quote from these films that are relevant to emotional detachment.]

PPT 64

Some good quotes from Epictetus

PPT 65

Even the Emperor can get job after *Star Wars!*

PPT 66

May the Force be With You This Xmas!

Chapter 37

Your Lack of Faith

Highly Classified Information – FYEO

The following evidence contains two exhibits.

Exhibit One – Leaked summary of the reply received to Allen's second Jedi workshop proposal.

Exhibit Two – Allen's response to rejection.

Psychological profile: Final exhibit shows initial stages of ego depletion despite operant conditioning's production of blind conformity toward dominant hierarchy. In layman's terms, he pissed.

Exhibit One

Rejected Tue 16/12/2008 – Due to the "rather problematic nature of the publicity surrounding the Jedi course before."

However Queen's University is "most keen to receive alternative proposals." Allen is held "in great esteem" for his "imaginative approach and dedication."

[Note – What they mean by this is the Welsh Jediism brothers who wanted to come over and debate me.]

Exhibit Two

From: Allen Baird [mailto:allen@sensei-winbeforehand.co.uk]

Sent: 17 December 2008 23:45

To: XXXX XXXX

Subject: RE: course proposals

Hello XXXX

Please find enclosed two new proposals to replace those that were rejected. Thanks you for giving me the opportunity to reapply.

Regarding the rejection of my second Jedi course proposal, I suppose I find myself somewhat confused as to why the nationwide publicity QUB received might be classed as 'problematic'. Although it consumed a fair whack of my time, I thought it was worth it to promote the OLP[11] and myself. However, the ways of the public sector are mysterious to those in the private. No hard feelings. And about the health and safety aspect to the other course [on self-protection], I understand, indeed I preempted your concerns. I have therefore modified it to remove any physical element, and made it about assertiveness and conflict resolution solely. I hope this is OK. Thanks for enrolling me on the two 1-day courses in March. I received conformation today.

Cordially

Allen

---

[11] Open Learning Programme

Chapter 38

Sware By No Greater

My name is Mark Gilmartin Black. It is Wednesday 31 December 2008. Here are my ten commandments for 2009.

1. I shall require no other resources but my own.
2. I shall remake my world in my own image.
3. My name will reveal who I chose to become.
4. I shall never rest.
5. I shall honour my own path to here.
6. I shall not hate my life as it is.
7. I shall not betray myself.
8. I shall not depend on the works of others.
9. I shall deceive everyone but myself.
10. I shall not yearn to be other than I am.

Signed: ~~Mark Black~~   **Darth Obsidian**

Sounds a bit *severe*, I know, but guess what, it's how I feel.

The Sith surname connects to my last name in an obvious way, and Deep Space Nine's Garak was the only alien I could ever stand. Also, I appreciate the associations with volcanoes, arrowheads, human sacrifices, skulls and scalpels. What self-respecting Darth wouldn't?

There, I'm doing it again, the whole tongue-in-cheek thing. I'm going to have to stay more in the idiom and leave behind this knowing, post-modern, 'Yes, I realise I'm not a real Darth' mentality. What's the point of being a Darth if you can't *be* a Darth? The title by itself conveys certain power and dignity. But if the *nom de guerre* is not serious, then neither are the attributes that emanate from it.

From now on, you will hear me speak with a different voice.

My chosen voice.

The voice of Darth Obsidian.

Cue evil cackle.

Stop it, me! You've got to cut the irony out.

Such are the trials of a dark lord of the Sith.

You've done it again, me! And you're making me speak to myself in a most Gollum-like fashion. That is not good.

Ok, alright. I need some practice is all.

I need some further training.

Chapter 39

He That Has Ears

Blog by Allen on 12 January 2009.

Star Wars **Goes To Work**

On December 9th (Belfast) and 10th (Dublin) I spoke at the Christmas Event of the *Institute of Internal Auditors* (Irish District Society). It was an exciting and challenging experience, since I've never done anything quite like it before. But the feedback from both events was excellent, with participants sending me emails of appreciation and request for more information.

Like the title of this blog, the presentation was called *Star Wars Goes to Work*. My subtitle sheds a bit more light on the content: *How to Use Jedi Mind-Tricks in Your Job to Get Your Way, Become Indispensable, and Stay Sane.* In it I offered tasters on topics like assertiveness and empathy at work ("how to get your way"), creativity and concentration ("how to become indispensable"), and emotional self-care and control ("how to stay sane").

This is how the talks were described in the promotional material.

"The presenter, Dr Allen Baird, a well-known communications guru, runs Sensei Learning and Performance, a Training, Coaching, Writing consultancy based in Belfast. He also delivers the short course *Feel the Force: How to Train in the Jedi Way*, at Queen's University Belfast, which aims to teach the real-life psychological techniques behind Jedi mind tricks. Dr. Baird's presentation will cover empathy and non-verbal communication, influencing and persuasion skills, and aims to deliver a serious message behind a fun image."

And this is what they said about me.

"Allen Baird PhD is a Partner in *Sensei Learning and Performance*, a Belfast based training, writing and coaching consultancy. Allen specialises in the design and delivery of management training and personal development workshops. He also consults on Emotional Intelligence, as well as issues related to business ethics and gender awareness. Allen is a qualified tutor at Queen's University Belfast, an award-winning public speaker, and a business advisor for Young Enterprise. He enjoys writing business blogs and making learning fun."

I thanked them for this flattering - if slightly unbelievable - introduction... I would like to thank those who organized these events, as well as the audiences, for their invitation, welcome and enthusiastic attention. An auditor is literally one who listens, a hearer. What better sort of audience could any speaker ask for?

Chapter 40

J is for Jedi

Classified Information – FYEO
General email sent to Queen's University from Hitul Thobhani of
kidz4mation followed by a children's story from Allen that is
allegedly autobiographical in nature.

From: Hitul Thobhani
Sent: 27 January 2009 11:09
To: Switchboard
Subject: Allen Baird

Hello

I wonder if you can help? I am trying to get in touch with Allen
Baird, a course tutor at QUB. Allen ran a course 'How to train in
the Jedi' that provoked our interest.

We are developing personal development programmes for children and would very much like to talk to Allen to share ideas. I would be grateful if you could send us his contact details.

Thanks and kind regards

Hitul & Seema Thobhani

Once upon a time there was a boy called Allen.

Allen was sad because he thought that other boys and girls could do things that he couldn't.

They could understand what the teacher said first time. Allen tried to understand but often gave up and daydreamed instead. They could spell long words and do sums in their heads. Allen had to copy others or write it down as best he could.

They could finish their homework quickly. Allen's younger brother Paul was smart and finished his homework before Allen even though he was two years younger!

No one told Allen why he had to go to school or what it was all about. It was just something you had to do because the big people said so.

The teacher thought Allen had something wrong with him. She called in Allen's parents to see her.

"Is Allen deaf?" she said.

One day they sent Allen away to see a special doctor when he was only seven. She tested Allen and asked him many questions and wrote everything down.

"He's a clever boy after all," she said. Allen didn't believe her.

When Allen was nine he saw a movie called *Star Wars*. He was with his parents visiting friends. They told him he could sit and watch the film with his brother. It was the best film ever! Allen wished it was real.

When Allen was ten he took a very important test. Allen failed the test and went to a different school from his friends. Allen hated school and books. Allen was angry and didn't want to learn another thing.

In the big school, Allen didn't study for exams. No-one showed him how. But Allen didn't care. You don't need exams to be a soldier, Allen thought.

Allen wanted to wear a uniform and shoot a gun and have adventures. He joined the army cadets to start him off. But all they wanted to do was get drunk and shout orders. They made Allen miserable.

Then, one day, when Allen was on holidays, he bought a comic. He only bought it because he was bored. Allen never read anything he didn't have to. But there was nothing else to do and he didn't want to sit in the sun any more. The comic was fantastic!

When Allen got home, he ordered a new comic every week. The best part of the week was reading that comic in a room by himself. They were not children's comics. They made Allen think about life and learn new words.

Soon Allen moved on from comics to books. They were not schoolbooks. They told stories about heroes like Luke Skywalker and villains like Darth Vader who lived on far away planets and battled each other. Sometimes Allen was sad that he didn't live on one of those planets.

As Allen grew up, he read all sorts of books. Some of these books were hard to read at first but Allen stuck at it because he enjoyed the stories so much. Most of Allen's old school friends and didn't read anymore, even the smart ones, but Allen kept reading,

reading and reading.

One day, Allen found out that he could read books and understand words that most others couldn't. This surprised Allen and made him wonder if he was smart after all and what smart meant.

One day some important people decided that Allen really was smart, so smart that they called him Doctor Allen. It made Allen scratch his head and ask how he suddenly became smart after being stupid for so long.

When Allen was all grown up, he often wondered if there were many boys who said they were stupid but weren't. It made Allen angry that schools only taught one way to be smart when there were many different ways. Allen thought how brilliant it would be to show these boys that they were without even knowing it.

Allen thought of Luke Skywalker, who was a simple farm boy until Obi-Wan showed him what to do. Luke could do many things he didn't even know he could do! Sometimes Luke was a bad pupil but he got there in the end. Luke then became a teacher so he could help others.

What Allen wished the most was that someone like Obi-Wan had helped him. Allen felt sad that he had to explain everything to himself and it made him tired. His best teachers were comics and films and books. Allen often dreamed about training some young Luke Skywalkers. If Allen could do that, he could live happy ever after.

Chapter 41

Cannot be Serious

Blog by Allen on 22 April 2009.

May the (Police) Force be With You!

More Jedi news - eight police officers serving with Scotland's largest force listed their official religion as Jedi in voluntary diversity forms. All this after some guy taught the UK's first Jedi course at Queen's University, Belfast. Why do these people do it? Is there any reason to take *Star Wars* so seriously?

First, there's the Jedi census phenomenon of 2001 in which 0.7% of the population of England and Wales classified themselves as Jedi. This made it the fourth largest religion in the country.

Second, there was role of *Star Wars* as a ground-breaking film. Much of the stuff we take for granted today - special effects, surround sound, the franchise picture, trilogies, genre mixing, comic-book style movies with happy endings - began with *Star Wars*. And the music was cool too!

Third, there is the cultural impact of *Star Wars*. Many of the phrases and references are embedded in the public psyche. Ronald Reagan named a missile defence system after it. There was (is?) even a 'Project Jedi' in the US military to create super-soldiers.

Beyond this, much could be said about philosophy and religion in *Star Wars*, and the meaning of the Force. It is a certainly a story with timeless, archetypal motifs and characters: an orphan, a magic sword, a princess to rescue, an evil wizard, a wise mentor, various strange monsters. George Lucas drew heavily from the "hero's journey" structure of Joseph Campbell. Luke Skywalker or Harry Potter (or indeed Frodo Baggins or King Arthur) ... what's the difference?

I think there are also interesting ethical and political issues raised by the *Star Wars* story. Rebels or freedom-fighters; separatists or rebels? Weapons of mass destruction. Instinct versus technology. Genetics and cybernetics. Single mothers and fatherless families. Destiny and choice. Egoism versus altruism. Dark energy and a single, unified Force. The 'father wound' and the 'shadow side' of human nature. It's all in there. And it's not hard to see.

So why would someone classify themselves as a Jedi? Because abundance is not enough. We need meaning in our lives. Stories are one of the main ways of giving this meaning, perhaps the oldest way. We need to feel part of something bigger than ourselves. We need to identify with the stories. We need to feel the force of being alive.

This isn't just for the nostalgic or the nerdy. It's part of being human. Probably the greatest part.

Whether you call it Jedi or something else is up to you.

Chapter 42

He Awaits But For the Dorn

Mauds Cafe, Ballyclare.

Thusday 23 April 2009, 19:30.

Allen meets businessman Derek Hall of EO Creative to discuss a joint venture.

Derek suggests they collaborate in designing an iPhone App to teach Jedi skills.

Allen has no idea what an iPhone App might be but draws out a first draft anyway.

How to do the Jedi Mind Tricks thing (intro)

1

Female Computer Voice: You have selected Jedi training holo-app zero one zero one point one. Please press to continue.

Graphics: As if viewer is looking at a Star Trek style control panel of a hand-held device, with various buttons and options.

2

Male Voice (mine): Greetings, Jedi apprentice. I am Master Dorn. I will guild you through this holo-app training module.

Graphics: A graphic representation of me as a Jedi, 'as if' I was a 3-D hologram, speaking to them personally.

[**Note** – I haven't decided on a Jedi name yet. This was the first one I thought of, thanks to Sheri S Tepper's excellent *The True Game* trilogies, which have stuck in my mind.]

3

Me: I remind you that its purpose is to support your training at our Jedi temple and with your own master, not to replace them. Action is our greatest teacher in the ways of the Force.

Graphics: The Jedi temple, with younglings training under instruction from a master, then perhaps some Knights with their padawan learners.

4

Me: You have chosen a training application about Jedi mind skills. Those not sensitive to the ways of the Force call them 'mind tricks.' From their viewpoint, they speak half a truth. These skills are not deceptions. But they are techniques that we Jedi can hone to our advantage.

Graphics: An anonymous Jedi (or me) performing the classic 'mind trick' with an alien while on a mission, complete with hand movement.

5

Me: First, padawan, you must understand this. Some Force powers have no parallel in the ordinary abilities of sentient beings. No amount of training can teach such a one to move this droid, or predict what will come through this access panel. We call these the Greater Abilities.

Graphics: An anonymous Jedi (or me) in a few 'action scenes.' First – using telekenesis to throw an enemy droid away. Then – a Jedi using precognition, waiting with lightsaber at ready as an enemy creature comes through a door.

6

Me: Other Force abilities are an enhancement of the skills we already possess. Jumping, balancing, aiming and falling are actions that anyone can perform. But with the Force, I have a strength, poise, accuracy, and resilience that far exceed the natural in scale.

What the Force does is magnify my natural abilities to a supernatural degree. We call these the Lesser Abilities.

Graphics: A Jedi using the Force to leap on to a high girder type structure, maintaining balance while under fire from a spherical seeker (like Luke practiced with), reflecting its fire back at it so it is destroyed, then somersaulting down a great height and landing on his feet.

7

Me: Many know this. Yet they remain unmindful of a further mystery.

Graphics: Me speaking to reader, torso and head, a warning finger raised to show the seriousness of the point.

8

Me: Imagine this. Before you are three smugglers. One has 10 credits; the second has 100 credits; and the third has 1000 credits. They learn of some villainous scheme to increase their credits twofold. Each receives a double measure, equally.

The method is the same for all. But the amount of credits each receives is not the same. Neither is the result. The first finishes with 20, the second 200, and the third 2000.

Graphic: Show three shady characters of the 'Mos Eisley Cantina' type standing before the reader. Make it look from left to right as if the first is poor, the second creature is average, and the last is rich. (For example, make the first skinny, droopy, while the third fat, confident, and well clothed.)

9

Me: So it is with the Force.

In the case of these natural abilities, the Force multiplies what skill-levels we already have. A regular pilot will become brilliant, while an already exceptional pilot will fly with a skill that easily exceeds the possible. This same principle applies to all physical prowess, whether with hand, eye or sabre.

Graphics: Images of mediocre then exceptional pilot tricks. Then shots of Jedi using skills of strength (physically throwing back a heavy enemy), perception (spotting an enemy walking out of a bar as the Jedi stands and looks around) and sabre craft (Jedi practising with traditional swords).

10

Me: Think of the Force as a lens that enlarges to a greater degree whatever is there already.

Graphics: Illustrate above with use of magnifying glass type lens. Maybe a Jedi looking into electro-binoculars as did Luke in *A New Hope* when looking for R2-D2.

11

Me: The better you are now, the better you will become with the Force.

Graphics: Me talking, even closer than 7, so show increasing revelation of mystery and seriousness of point.

12

Me: This not only concerns skills of the body. It also applies to our minds.

Graphics: Jedi in meditation pose. (Contrast with earlier action graphics.)

13

Me: The truth I speak of is less well known, since mental skills are harder to name and harder to learn than physical or even technical skills. They are therefore often ignored by traditional education in most planetary systems, to their detriment.

Graphics: Show a fat schoolboy (contemporary Earth) trying to run or climb in a school gymnasium. Then show a bored schoolgirl (contemporary earth) sitting in her room doing some science homework whole looking wistfully out the window at the moon and stars.

14

Me: Rare exceptions to this include primitive attempts to harness the power of the mind through ascetic discipline or mystical observances.

Graphics: Show Buddhist (Shaolin?) type monk, cross-legged, cleaning his sword, and a Knight Templar in prayer in a church (with sword and armour on).

15

Me: Or through ancient scientific research into the paranormal. Judged by our standards now, their attempts, while laudable, seem to us little better than alchemy did to them.

Graphics: Show earth hippies with crystals, candles, in a circle, smoking pot, with a copy of *Zen and the Art of Motorcycle Maintenance* lying around etc.

16

Me: In your people's ancient history, there was an interesting exception to this amateur quest. It came, not from the realms of religion or research, but commerce and trade.

Graphics: Me walking from a temple scene into a market place.

17

Me: Some of the first to take what mind-skills they had and apply them to life in an effective way were merchants. It is easy to guess why. Selling, negotiating and motivating are the lifeblood of business. What war was to their bodies, custom was to their minds.

Graphics: Businesspeople (contemporary earth) taking to each other, making deals, giving presentations and sales pitches, in planning meetings and marketing teams etc.

18

Me: Many were driven by a profit motive, true, and an attempt to gain advantage over their competitors. But others used business as a non-violent theatre in which to develop their own potentials.

Graphics: One fat businessman with a calculator, looking down at it. Another beside him with book, holding it to his chest, smiling. Maybe skyscrapers in the middle.

19

Me: A class of teachers arose within their ranks who educated them in these mind-skills. Then, they called them *trainers* or *coaches*.

They most closely resemble the *senseis* and *gurus* of even more ancient times that have now passed into legend. Yet the methods of these trainers was a great advance in Force-awareness, however feeble their powers seem now to us with our fuller knowledge of the living Force.

Graphics: Two (cotemporary Earth) businessmen in discussion, sitting, facing each other, nothing in between. One, leaning forward, looks to be asking a question. The other sits back, reflective, looking up.

20

Me: Padawan, there are six of their mind-skills I will now reveal to you. These ancient trainers knew them in their basic forms. So the principles upon which they are based are very old. We have a more perfect knowledge, yes. But even yet, with us, their meaning and methods are much less understood than those physical skills that are usually identified with the Jedi.

That is why you are here to learn of them, is it not?

Graphics: Me, hands up, in an explaining posture. Then, pointing to reader.

21

Me: As a Jedi, you must understand that the mind and body are connected together as one living system. Each is a perspective on the other. You must master these skills of the mind just as you master your body. Only then can you can master your weapons and your fighter-ship. Your success in any mission, your very life, will depend on both.

Graphic: The outline of a human form, but split in half. One half shows the physical, biological side makeup of man. The other, a spiritual, 'energy' view.

22

Me: Remember the image of the smugglers with their credits, apprentice. The greater your skill now, the more the Force can magnify those skills when you need them.

Graphic: A Jedi fighting the three smugglers from 8 (using mind methods to fling them about or psych them out).

23

Me: It is the purpose of this holo-app to introduce six of these mind-skills to you.

Further holo-apps will expand on each. In these, which you can access later, I will demonstrate them, one at a time. I will provide exercises to enable you to practice them at your own leisure. And I will suggest missions for you to test and improve your skill levels.

Graphic: Me handing out a comp-pad with a mission on it to the reader.

24

Me: Let us begin our brief introduction.

The six mind-skills you need to develop are sensitivity, persuasion, flow, control, intuition, empathy.

Graphic: As each is mentioned, there comes up a symbol or action for each.

[**NOTE** – I haven't decided on the order of these yet. But at this stage it doesn't matter too much.]

25

Me: Sensitivity is the state of feeling those small changes in your environment that others take for granted. This involves both a heightened use of the tradition five senses, and a conscious deployment of those beyond, such as your senses of balance, acceleration, pain and bodily position.

Graphic: A graphic of each of these senses. Perhaps a Jedi using them in some heightened way.

26

Me: Persuasion is the skill of influencing others to perform actions that they might not otherwise choose. Instead of coercion and strength, the persuader uses the power of words, voice and behaviour as a means of affecting the minds of other beings.

Graphics: A Jedi in conversation with a creature, possibly an interrogation, forceful pointing by the Jedi, the creature giving information.

27

Me: Flow is the experience of focused and deep concentration when you perform some activity. If your skill matches the challenge, mind will merge with action so that you perform it with an unconscious ease.

Graphics: A Jedi piloting a craft through a terrific manoeuvre with a look of ease, or using a sabre with the same look of calm.

28

Me: Control is your ability to exercise power over your own mental states, cleansing yourself of rage, fear, despair and other emotions we Jedi class as negative. Such self-management requires a high level of mindfulness in our assessment of our own pressure points and triggering mechanisms.

Graphics: A Jedi in a high stress situation, maybe where others are panicking or angry (like a bar room brawl that is about to start). The Jedi remains unflappable.

29

Me: Empathy is the capability to connect with others so that you understand their motives and frame of reference. Such mind tuning is accomplished by careful observation of what is communicated to us beyond words, such as (for the human species) small facial expressions, eye movements and other indicators.

Graphics: A Jedi focusing on the face of someone with a highly intensive look.

30

Me: Intuition is way of shortcutting usual methods of receiving information and decision-making. By drawing from preconscious sources of knowledge, we can pick up danger signals or spot a deception in an instant of time, when there is no time for a process of reasoning.

Graphics: A Jedi reacting to a dangerous trap in an instant, so not falling into it.

31

Me: Those non Force-users who possess a high level of ability in these six mind-skills differ from the ordinary almost as much as we Jedi differ from them. The gap is like that between a planet-class athlete and the casual spectator.

Graphics: Two people facing the reader. Same people though they undergo here changes of clothes and context. Scene 1 – ordinary guy on left, more 'heroic' guy on right. Scene 2 – guy on right become a Jedi. Scene three – guy on right becomes an athlete.

32

Me: Consider, then, padawan, how much you may gain from their mastery. Without them, but with the Force as your ally, you may yet earn the rank of Jedi Knight. But with them, and with the Force, you will become a Jedi Master of renown.

Graphics: Compare Jedi Knight with a Master sitting on the council.

33

Me: You will do well, padawan, to consider these things before you activate the next holo-app.

Graphic: Me speaking to reader is a warning posture.

34

Me: It is not enough for a Jedi to possess a memory store of information about the history, structure, and lore of our order. A computer could match that achievement. A Knight of vision will focus on those matters that are harder, or impossible, for mere machines to duplicate.

Graphics: A (contemporary earth) kid being guided by me to leave down his SW novels or website to go outside into the world!

35

Me: It is not sufficient for a Jedi to spend a lifetime mastering the physical disciplines and martial styles that characterise our order. A being equipped with enhancement technologies or bioengineering could overcome performance limitations to a similar degree. Knights with experience will allow for this reality, and prepare their apprentices for it.

Graphics: A Jedi (me??) fights a Boba Fett type enemy who is also levitating etc.

36:

Me: Your preparation begins now, my young apprentice. Farewell for now.

Graphics: We giving farewell gesture, as a small figure in larger Jedi temple background.

37
Female Computer Voice: Jedi training holo-app zero one zero one point one is complete. Please press to exit.

Graphics: As with 1.

Chapter 43

You Will Be Assimilated

Common Grounds Cafe, Belfast.
Tuesday 28 July 2009, 2:30 pm.
Allen sits at a table, drinking a middle-class beverage.

We meet at my request.

I was working on another project entirely, a conference on storytelling, innovation and business called, appropriately, *Storytelling, Innovation and Business*. It is my job to seek out strange new training topics, in this case showcasing local talent who could contribute a session or two on the subject.

I Googled some relevant words and his name found its way to near the top: Rory O'Connor. That's how I do my market research. If you're not on Google you don't exist.

He is a trainer like me, and about the same age (mid-thirties, to be imprecise). His claim to fame so far was that he has

217

developed a set of nine six-sided dice with a different symbol on each. You roll the dice and find hints to aid your creative thinking and problem solving. These he imaginatively brands as *Rory's Story Cubes*. They'd gotten him on TV at least once, so again, same as me.

What really caught my eye was the fact that he mentioned *Star Wars* on his website. 'I describe myself as being of the *Star Wars* generation, growing up with the universal energy of *The Force* on the one hand, and the practical down-to-earth problem solving of MacGyver on the other.' Personally, I can't stand MacGyver. I hate it when dumb, blonde-haired people are allowed by producers to act smart, by virtue of an up-beat theme and a Swiss army knife. I owned such a knife as a boy and it didn't make me smart, or blond, still hasn't. Patty and Selma can have him. MacGyver, that is, not Rory.

It was clear to me from his website that he knew plenty of stuff that I didn't know. This was a good omen for me. I didn't want someone on board who would repeat what I already said. I was after someone with a different perspective on the whole Jedi thing. I got this in spades from Rory. He has qualifications in Non-Violent Communication, nice enough, but also in subjects with strange words like Guided Self-Healing, Emotional Freedom Technique, and Spiral Dynamics. I'm always impressed when someone mentions subject matter and I don't know what the feck they're talking about. Is that a weakness or a strength?

When I think of Rory I name him the Irish Jedi. Now I'm Irish in the sense of Northern Irish. What that means is that my ancestors have lived here from when Galileo first made his observations but we still don't quite think of ourselves as natives.

We're really British, see, even though they, the British, call us Paddies and sing *While Irish Eyes Are Smiling* when they're drunk on foreign holidays to make us feel better. Don't ask.

Rory is the real Irish deal. For starters, if you had to invent a name that sounded as Irish as you could make it, apart from Paddy O'Neill, you couldn't do better than Rory O'Connor. Then there are his looks. The golden hair (which is a nice way of saying ginger). The generous freckles. The twinkly blue eyes. The potato shaped head. (I made that last one up.) It's all there. If he had a real lightsaber, it would surely vibrate with an awesome emerald green.

Then he opens his mouth and talks and the stereotypes take a speeder out towards the rim of the rainbow along with the crock of dilithium. Yes, he has the accent, more than me, but that's all. His voice is soft and calm, understated even. His seriousness of mind measures approximately eight point six on the Solemnity Scale, compared to my own fairly impressive seven point nine. (I used to be nine point one but then I got married.) Yet a smile usually plays near the edges of his mouth, darting around the room with his gaze. I haven't seen him drink Guinness or play the fiddle once. He's a smart, creative guy.

On the day we met, I was strictly on the lattés myself, and the only music around was *Just Like You Imagined* when my mobile deigned to announce a caller.

It was one of those lightly awkward first meetings you get used to when you run your own Small-to-Medium Enterprise. I'm a little before time, he's a little after, that's fine.

He cycled and I came by car. Usually I don't trust people who cycle, it's such a politician's thing to do, and I count politicians as a subspecies of parasite more ancient than

219

paragonimus westermani. As Rory didn't attempt to pump my hand with a power-shake, I bracketed my prejudices away for future use.

If you had to select the potential politician between us, more than likely you would have pointed at me. I was wearing a high-quality suit (there were no shiny, balding patches or anything), writing with a silver pen, supping American coffee with a brief agenda written out on my Moleskine notebook, all proportionately placed out before me on the table.

Albert Mehrabian would have been proud of me that morning. Rory seemed indifferent but not in a bad sense. He's the sort of bloke who, if you look hard enough into his pupils, you can see the wheels whirling around behind, forming new conjunctions, creating fresh neural pathways.

That's OK too; I've met enough mirror-men to last my life cycle.

I talked first about my conference and the sort of speakers I sought. We spent some time on his story cubes. He gave me a free demo. I was half-convinced there and then, which is well done to him since for me doubt is not so much an attitude to life as a methodological starting point for all things. *Dubito ergo sum.*

I asked him a legion of questions about the other areas in which he specialises. I prefer asking questions, although many times I go overboard and end up making the recipient feel more like the accused in a kind of unexpected Spanish Inquisition. In the virtuous circle of conversation, there is *tell* as well as *ask.*

We move on to *Star Wars.* We touch on the possibility of a joint venture. I tell him that I need people who have abilities and can train in topics that I can't. One Allen is enough. He thought he

220

was such a one, though not *the* One obviously. So we arranged another meet-up for a few weeks' time.

We're both busy chaps you know.

Chapter 44

Comb-over Kings

Common Grounds Cafe Belfast.
Friday 7 August, 2009, 11:30 am.
Allen again waits for Rory.

I have a secret weakness in this whole Jedi training venture that I don't know how to overcome. The Force. I don't know what to do with the Force.

There was a guy I talked to in a previous vocational incarnation who claimed to believe in 'God or the Force or something'. That's one possibility but one I don't like. The Judeo-Christian concept of God is of an Absolute Person who is wholly distinct from the cosmos. The Force seems to be impersonal, a thing, an energy field created by all living things. But God is uncreated. True, the Force seems to have a will, which is a necessary condition of personhood. Yet Jedi do not talk to the Force or relate to the Force in a personal way. They *use* the Force. In my limited understanding, God is above exploitation or manipulation by acolytes.

If I wanted to trek through the maze of Force = God I'd contact as a guide a guy called Stevie Patterson, a Christian youth worker whose wife is a dead ringer for Mara Jade Skywalker. That kind of makes him Luke Skywalker, and together they could rule the universe as husband and wife. Plus she just gave birth to twins, which is well *Star Wars*-y, even though they were born of May the second instead of the fourth. The only problem with Stevie is that he finds people's lack of faith disturbing. This is a blatant dark side trait.

Second on my usual suspects list is *chi*, which is usually translated as *life-force* or *energy flow*. Whichever translation you prefer, if you're into *Star Wars* and you hear words like that, your antennae *ping*. But here's the rub. I've tried to keep my Jedi training rigorously within the Western world of psychology even when tempted to wander eastward (for example when teaching about mindfulness). Why? I don't know much about it beyond what I gleaned from watching *Kung Fu* with David Carradine as a kid and recently reading *The Complete Idiots Guide to Taoism*. What I do know is Western philosophy, which brings me to my third candidate.

There is a position called *vitalism* that holds that there is more to life than the laws of Physics and Chemistry. The French philosopher Henri Bergson named this extra element the *élan vital* or life force and linked it to consciousness itself. Variations of this are Mesmer's 'animal magnetism' and Freud's 'psychic energy'. A more extreme version of this is called *hylozoism*, a belief that even

223

material thinks; rocks and X-wing fighters possess a sort of life, since life and matter are interrelated.

While I find these ideas fascinating, I also judge them unhelpful in putting together a Jedi workshop. They are heavily intellectual and abstract. I can imagine a classroom full of eyes start to glaze over once I answer the question, 'Is that were we get the word mesmerise from?,' in the affirmative. You can't *do* anything with these theories except discuss whether they are true or false. I also have a natural aversion to all things hippy, possibly unwarranted, but my appraisal of free love is as a getting-laid strategy for fifty-something-year-old college lecturers. I was raised in the 80's, where Hollywood taught us to respect Vietnam vets rather than project spoilt-rich-kid saliva at them.

These are my thoughts as I wait to meet Rory again. Last time, he mentioned a book called *The Field* by Lynne McTaggart, a book that tried to link clairvoyants with physicists. I've done a bit of background research and I'm feeling mildly uneasy. The subtitle is *The Quest for the Secret Force of the Universe*. Yes, it looks like an enjoyable read but so is *Watchmen*. Yes, science can't explain everything; I've read my Kuhn and Feyerabend. Yes, Western medicine often seems little more than a pimp for the pharmaceuticals industry. But that's still a millennial stretch away from homeopathy, energy medicine, and spiritual healing.

He comes in, sits down, and we get stuck into business. He's out to persuade an old cynic like me. Rory starts with the Unified Field Theory but I've heard of it already, who hasn't. (That's a joke, cool down.) He then moves on to Dissonance Theory and the emergent nature of life. Interesting, yes, but the immediate relevance escapes me. We have a debate about the manipulative powers of empathy and body language. I inform him that I'm more of a Grey Jedi when it comes to those sort of issues, meaning that I think the techniques are neutral and can be used for good or ill. He seems uncomfortable with is notion, or maybe my joke isn't all that funny, just like the last one. I ask him what he would actually do with these ideas on the day of a joint Jedi training event.

At first, he mentions centering exercises, designed to focus your mind on the present time and the current location, attentive yet relaxed, controlled but open. Nice, I like it, but I could do it. I need more. He gives me more, way more. He leads me on another exercise with the intention of feeling something called 'subtle energy'. We engage in a spot of 'energy combing' as you do in the middle of a café. I'm polite and I'm curious and I don't give a monkey's if people stare so I run along with it.

Results were inconclusive, true, so I'm not sold on it yet. I'll have to read more, think more, experience more first. It's hard to judge where creative science ends and creative writing begins, if you take my meaning. But I am convinced that Rory is in touch with knowledge that I'm not, and that he would have a part to play in our pioneering event. He is a born teacher, lateral thinker and innovator.

So now there were two.

Chapter 45

The Nanotech Ninja

University of Ulster, office of Dr Colin Turner, Senior Lecturer, Nanotechnology and Advanced Materials Research Institute.
Thursday 13 August 2009, 10:15

One weakness in my Jedi training fantasies has always been my own lack of martial arts ability. As I said, I've done a little, but nothing near enough to count me as an experienced practitioner, never mind an instructor. And, let's face it, at a Jedi training event, that's what people want more than anything else. They want their own lightsaber and they want some master to show them how to use it. All the rest comes under the heading of 'nice but not necessary'.

What I'd really love at the event is a sword expert. I've vaguely heard about these guys. Film companies hire them to teach the basics to actors like Viggo Mortensen and John Terry who have to wield a vorpal blade against some manxome foe or other. I can't find any such person in Northern Ireland although I know a few chaps who are a dab hand with a sledgehammer if you oil them right on a Friday night. Some fencing master with breeches and thigh high socks, well, no thank-you. I appreciate French toast but I want my sword *at least* one inch thick and preferably double-handed.

As far as the unarmed combat aspect goes, I'm left with two Jedi-like options. One is to persuade a self-defence instructor to take the class through a few moves. Most people don't realise that self-defence and martial arts aren't the same. Self-defence includes a physical element but is just as much about personal security, avoidance and awareness, verbal and non-verbal conflict counter-measures. The hard-to-hand aspect is reality-based, without any sports aspect, designed for survival rather than style. My brother-in-law Matthew Arrell is a self-defence instructor and would help me for free. We've worked together before with great success.

The other option is for an Aikido instructor to come and lead us in a few techniques. I don't know much about Aikido beyond the fact that Stephen Segal was an Aikido Master prior to becoming a water-horse (by that I mean 'hippopotamus' but I don't want to meet him when I'm on my way up and he's on his way down and for him to say, "Are you the guy that called me a big, fat hippo?" *Smack!*).

What I do know is that Aikido is as much a philosophy of inner harmony as a martial art, and that it's a 'soft' style that requires little physical strength or aggression

With this jumble of thoughts in mind, I go to Google, click in some words and see what pops up.

There aren't too many Aikido instructors in Northern Ireland, which is helpful in narrowing down my field of search. I limit it again to those who live in the Belfast area to make it easier on myself should I want to pay them a visit. Again, I want someone with proper accreditation and maybe a website I can snoop around. After all this, I come across the name of Colin Turner.

Colin is a Second Dan in traditional Aikido. His club has a website. Better still, *he* has a website. *Ka-ching!* I've hit the information jackpot. Now I can see what sort of bloke this Colin is before I even meet him. Not only is he an Aikido instructor, he also teaches Japanese swordsmanship or *Iaido*. *Bing!* He's a university lecturer with a PhD. *Ba-Da-Bing!* His hobbies include reading science fiction and role-playing games. *Ba-Da-Boom!* I think I've just found an ideal candidate.

After a few emails, we arrange to meet up at his campus office.

On the day, once I work my around the labyrinth of floors and corridors, we finally meet up.

In physical appearance, I estimate he could pass for a Northern Irish version of Christian Bale. What this means in practice is that he looks a *little* like Christian Bale if you squint your eyes and drink four tins of Stella. He's not Hollywood handsome or what my dad would call a pretty boy. So he's not *really* like Bale, although I wouldn't comment to either of them about their looks. They could both beat my head in.

His speaking volume is slightly louder than average, in this case, me being the average. All his words come forth at the same rate, with the same tone, like a computer outputting information. When explaining anything, he goes back to basics and definitions.

Each sentence follows on from the other. There is sequence and structure here; like me, he talks as one might write a research paper. Most of my friends have the same ability, or is it disorder. This tells you something about my friends and the fun we have at weekends.

I give him my vision for the day. He seems neither enthused nor incredulous. We discuss Aikido and he demonstrates a few moves. He explains his art well, moving back and forth between principle and praxis. True, no one will ever pigeonhole him as laconic. But a teacher needs to be comfortable talking, explaining, elucidating. I know I can trust him to organise his sessions and keep his bottle before a large crowd. That is as important to me as the *Hong Kong Phooey*. And he's as smart as a whip, or in this case, a *shinken*.

We arrange to meet with Rory at his dojo and observe him in action. Colin, that is, not Rory. Watching Rory *think* would scarce constitute a quality night's entertainment. Watching anyone *think* would scarce constitute a quality night's entertainment. Unless they were Lex Luthor.

And even then.

Chapter 46

Shadows and Dust

Blog by Allen on 21 August 2009.

Mind Tricks and Mind Games

Apart from their use as a double-handed thing hitter, a lightsaber and a cricket bat don't seem to have too much in common.

But that's where you're wrong. For the skillful wielding of both, it is mind rather than muscle that wins the day. You will learn all about this at our Jedi Knight Training Event in October, where experts will instruct you on the proper use of the samurai sword, and the flash of lightsaber duels will electrify the afternoon air.

More details on this exciting event next week, but for now, let's go back to cricket. In an enlightening article called *The Ashes Mind Game,* a consultant psychologist shows how mind tricks are necessary for excellent performance in any field of action.

Here are the two insights I found the most interesting (italics mine).

"During the game the players need to *focus on the processes*…We wouldn't be having conversations with the players about the outcome and how it's going to feel at the end. It's more about what are we doing *today*, what do we need to execute *today* to put us in the strongest position possible to win this game, rather than the romantic dreams of what might be happening next Monday or Tuesday."

"Our focus is about us, about what we need to do, what we can control, how we can prepare and how we can position ourselves to start this game strongly… It's about controlling the controllables and *focusing on what you can do in our environment*."

We have a culture that emphasises goal-setting and planning as methods of gaining success. I strongly feel that we must balance this with a sense of mindfulness (awareness of the present) and flow (engagement with the present). I will be speaking on both these concepts at the forthcoming Jedi Training Event (with reference to *Star Wars*). Tenuous link?

Then hear the words of Martin Seligman: "Role models and paragons in the culture compellingly illustrate a strength or virtue. Models may be real (Mahatma Gandhi and humane leadership), apocryphal (George Washington and honesty), or explicitly mythic (Luke Skywalker and flow)." I'll never tire of quoting this line.

Or, as Yoda said about a young, excitable Luke: "This one a long time have I watched. Never his mind on where he was. Hmm? What he was doing. Hmph."

Dreams are good. But what are you doing right here, right now?

Chapter 47

Love Me Two Times

Blog by Allen on 24 August 2009.

Jedi Knight Training Event in Belfast!

This exciting 1-day workshop is a joint venture between me (Allen Baird of *Sensei Learning and Performance*) and Rory O'Connor of *The Creativity Hub.*

In 2008, I designed and delivered the UK's first university course teaching Jedi Skills. Held at Queen's University Belfast, where I am a tutor, the 1-day workshop gained coverage in *The Guardian Education Supplement*, *The Times Higher Education Supplement*, *The Times Online*, *The Daily Telegraph*, *The Irish News*, *The News Letter*, and BBC *News Online.* Called *Feel the Force: How to Train the Jedi Way*, we were also featured on international radio and local TV.

Our new event is timed to coincide with the *Invasion Belfast II* event held at W5 in the Odyssey in October this year.

Rory, creative thinking expert and creator of *Rory's Story Cubes*, will join me to offer Northern Ireland's most exciting-slash-only Jedi training event of 2009. Rory and I will explain the famous Jedi Mind-Trick by showing how to gain control over and from the minds of others. Rory will explore the subjects of Energy Psychology and Subtle Energy fields to gain modern insight in the mystical Force. I will then walk participants through the films to see those psychological skills Luke Skywalker gained in becoming a Jedi, and those Anakin lacked in his fall to the dark side.

Other special features of this workshop include a demonstration by Rory of the latest Jedi training technologies such as the Force Trainer. Also, local instructors will give a talk and demonstration on Aikido and Iaido. Aikido is a powerful martial art that emphasizes defence rather than attack, and means 'the way of harmony with life force'. Not known much in Ireland, Iaido is the Japanese art of drawing, striking with and sheathing the samurai sword.

As the highlight of the day, each participant will receive their own dueling lightsaber and have a chance to test what they have learned! This lightsabers are combat-durable - not the cheap, breakable ones you had as a kid. Especially imported from the US, these lightsabers are the closest you can get to wielding the real thing!

Our Jedi Training Facility for the day is the Conference Suite of the

Belfast Activity Centre, a personal development charity off the Malone Road in south Belfast. Ample, free car-parking space is available. It will take place on Saturday 17th October 2009 from 9 am to 5 pm.

Cost for the day is £77.50. This includes lunch, snacks, and tea/coffee throughout the day. Also included in the cost is a lightsaber, which every participant can take away with them.

Click here to book online and take your first step into a larger world.

If you book before 19th September, you can choose your lightsaber colour from blue, orange, green, red or silver. If you book after this, we will post your lightsaber out to you later.

To avoid disappointment, book early you must!

Chapter 48

Our Own Private Coruscant

Summary of New Jedi event on Eventbrite.

Jedi Knight Training Event

The Jedi are landing in Northern Ireland this October! In a joint venture between Allen Baird of Sensei Learning and Performance and Rory O'Connor of The Creativity Hub, these masters will train younglings and apprentices in the ways of the Force.

Allen has taught Jedi since 2008, when he designed and delivered the UK's first university course teaching Jedi Skills. Called *Feel the Force: How to Train the Jedi Way*, the event was also featured on international radio, national newspapers and local TV.

The Jedi syllabus for the day consists of four sessions.

Session 1: Jedi Mind Tricks – How to gain control over and from the minds of others using Assertiveness, Body Language and Non-Violent Communication techniques (Allen and Rory)

Session 2: Feel the Force – Training in Energy Psychology with the detection and manipulation of Subtle Energy fields, and an introduction to Force training technologies (Rory)

Session 3: Jedi Mental Skills – Luke's rise (growth in Sensitivity, Flow, and Empathy) and Anakin's downfall (failure in Balance, Mindfulness, and Detachment) over the six films (Allen)

Session 4: Jedi Martial Skills – Demonstrations by local experts in self-defence, samurai swordsmanship and basic lightsaber drills (Colin Turner and John Donaldson)

Our Jedi Training Facility for the day is the Conference Suite of the Belfast Activity Centre (Barnett's Stable Yard, Barnett Demesne, Malone Road, BT9 5PB).

Scheduled launch time is Saturday 17 October 2009 from 9 am to 5 pm.

Cost includes lunch, snacks, tea and coffee throughout the day, and a combat lightsaber.

If you book before 19 September, you can choose your lightsaber colour from blue, orange, green, red or silver. If you book after this, we will post your lightsaber out to you later.

Chapter 49
Let Me Go

Press Release for new Jedi event.

Jedi Training Event Strikes Back in Belfast
Two local training organisations are combining forces to teach
Northern Ireland the ways of the Jedi Knights. This unique 1-day
workshop is a joint venture between Dr Allen Baird of *Sensei
Learning and Performance and* Rory O'Connor of *The Creativity
Hub.*

In October 2008, Allen designed and delivered the UK's first
university course teaching Jedi Skills. Held at Queen's University
Belfast, where Allen is a tutor, the 1-day workshop gained coverage
in *The Guardian Education Supplement, The Times Higher
Education Supplement, The Times Online, The Daily Telegraph,
The Irish News, The News Letter, The South Belfast News,* and *BBC*

News Online. Called *Feel the Force: How to Train the Jedi Way*, the event was also featured on international radio and local TV.

Allen says, "The interest in my event last year was mind-blowing. Getting on UTV with David Prowse, the actor who played Darth Vader in the original films, was the highlight for me. This year we're taking it out of the university and into the community so everyone can have a go. Again, we're timing it to coincide with *Invasion Belfast II* at The Odyssey."

Rory, creative thinking expert and creator of *Rory's Story Cubes*, will join Allen to offer Northern Ireland's most exciting training event of 2009. Allen and Rory will explain the famous Jedi Mind-Trick by showing how to gain control over and from the minds of others. Rory will explore the subjects of Energy Psychology and Subtle Energy fields to gain modern insight in the mystical Force. Allen will walk participants through the films to see those psychological skills Luke Skywalker gained in becoming a Jedi, and those Anakin lacked in his fall to the dark side.

Other special features of this workshop include a demonstration by Rory of the latest Jedi training technologies such as the Force Trainer. Also, local instructors will give a talk and demonstration on Aikido and Iaido. Aikido is a powerful martial art that emphasizes defence rather than attack, and means 'the way of harmony with life force'. Not known much in Ireland, Iaido is the Japanese art of drawing, striking with and sheathing the samurai sword.

As the highlight of the day, each participant will receive their own dueling lightsaber and have a chance to test what they have learned! The lightsabers are combat-durable – not the cheap, breakable ones you had as a kid. Especially imported from the US, these lightsabers are the closest you can get to wielding the real thing!

Our Jedi Training Facility for the day is the Conference Suite of the Belfast Activity Centre, a personal development charity off the Malone Road in south Belfast. It will take place on Saturday 17th October 2009 from 9 am to 5 pm.

Chapter 50

Knights in White Satin

Cregagh Youth & Community Centre,
Mount Merrion Avenue, Belfast.
Wednesday 26 Aug 2009, 7:30 pm.

I'm a few minutes late for a change and the action has already started. Rory is there, squatting on his haunches in the corner of the matted hall, sketching diagrams of moves.

Most impressive.

Already, Colin is *in flagrante delicto* with some half dozen students, all wearing traditional Japanese *kakama*, except for one newcomer in a tracksuit.

There's something agreeable in having not too many in a martial arts class. I've attended ju-jitsu training before with over thirty per night. Fortune smiled on you if you received thirty seconds personal attention from the instructor per hour. This way, you get value for time.

After a nod to me, Colin divides the class up in terms of experience and sets them appropriate techniques to try out. He works a little more with the newest comers. Like all good instructors, he makes it look easy. In fact, you only realise how difficult some of the moves are when others try to do them.

Aikido is a graceful art when performed well.

What impresses me is Colin's attempt to keep the training real. Elegance is fine in the safe confines of a dojo, but what about the street, the pub, the interspecies cantina? And when I say 'real' I mean Geoff Thompson type real. Now Colin didn't eff and blind, but it wasn't ballet either. Do you have a problem with that, sunshine?

Afterwards we went to a cafe to make our war plans. As Rory and Colin talked, one major question played on my mind. *If I'm 'Hannibal' (since it's my plan) and Colin is 'BA' (since he's the best fighter), then does that make Rory 'Murdock' or 'Face'?* His penchant for MacGyver pushes him towards the Templeton Peck side, but creativity and madness are related, as both involve looking at reality in new ways. A dilemma, then.

Well someone has to ask the tough questions.

Chapter 51

Hoffer Meets Hannibal

A squat somewhere in Belfast.

Sunday 20 August 2009, 7:28 am.

Mark sites in a chair, surrounded by books and papers.

My studies are progressing well. Beyond those masters Baird already pointed me toward, I have added Ayn Rand, Ragnar Redbeard, Cialdini, and Richard Dawkins. I'm forming my own Sith reading list. I salvage what I can from Neuro-linguistic Programming but it's a mixed bag as Baird himself admitted. As I read his blogs it surprises me how much we have in common.

I see he has begun to draw others to himself. A Weapons Master and a Force User. Wise choices for one who lacks the stomach for the first and the vision for the second. It wouldn't surprise me if he darkens a church door on Sunday and pays his taxes. *But is he a true believer, Eric?*

He aims to bring them all together for another training event. I foresee it will not succeed. His thinking is too conventional. The first course worked because of a happy coincidence of fortune for him. It was the first of its kind – a university course about *Star Wars*. And it fell on the same month as Northern Ireland's first *Star Wars* costumed convention. Serendipitous for Baird in the short term but in the long term it stunted his growth. Easy victory always does.

I'll hold off signing up for it until I see the size of the ripple it creates. If the waves are generous enough I can hide myself behind them.

I've started exercising again, running, free weights, pounding on a home-made punch bag. With every session, I can feel myself becoming stronger, more powerful. I'm on the lookout for a martial arts trainer who does private and deadly, none of that *Crouching Tiger, Hidden Dragon* bull. And every man needs his sword.

I'm losing weight, using food and sleep as my servants. I'm drawing up plans, timelines, imagining scenarios, weighing between alternatives. I'm reaching out but on my terms.

I'm done with the booze, the fags, the games, the drugs, the soaps, the cheap burgers, the untold dreams, the snivelling self-pity. My *Miniver Cheevy* days have ended.

I have not found a way. So I will make one.

Thus spoke Darth Obsidian.

Chapter 52

Apollo Moon Landings

Cregagh Youth & Community Centre,
Mount Merrion Avenue, Belfast.
Wednesday 2 September 2009, 7:28 pm.

Tonight I arrive at the dojo with Dawn and camera in tow. We're here before the start of Colin's class to take some publicity snaps.

I've spent the last few hours gathering together every scrap of potentially useable *Star Wars* merchandise I can lay my hands on. I've got a Stormtrooper Mask, three plastic lightsabers and a poster.

The others have done the same.

I could spend many words describing what happened over the next thirty minutes as we arranged our makeshift studio.

Instead, I'll show you the result and you can judge for yourselves.

That's Colin standing on the right. The other instructor on the left is called John Donaldson, *Star Wars* fan, doting father and all round hard man. Of the two kneeling down in the centre, I'll leave you to guess which one is Rory and which is me.

To my knowledge, no newspaper used our photo. Obviously yet another face-shot of Peter 'Robbo' Robinson is far more visually stimulating.[12]

---

[12] At point of writing, Northern Ireland's First Minister.

Chapter 53
Into Great Silence

Blog by Allen on 14 September 2009.

The Way of the Warrior Monk

I've been thinking about the Jedi again, and how they are a mythical type of the warrior-monk. Different cultures have expressed this type throughout the centuries: the Sohei warriors of ancient Japan, the Knights Templar, perhaps the Islamic Assassins, and definitely the Shaolin monks of Kung-Fu fame.

There is something attractive to me about this combination of seeming opposites. The war-maker and the peace-keeper. The 'this-worldly' and the 'other-worldly'.

Aristotle contrasted the 'contemplative life' with the 'active life', arguing in favour of the former; Aquinas followed his lead. Those in the Roman Catholic tradition make a similar contrast between the interior life and the exterior.

From the personal development viewpoint, there's something very familiar to me in all this. There are many such contrasts that need to be overcome in order to achieve something higher.

- Assertiveness Training - contrast between passive and aggressive (unified by assertiveness)
- Emotional Intelligence - contrast between self-smart and social-smart (unified by empathy)
- Transactional Analysis - contrast between child ego state and parent ego state (unified by the adult ego state)
- Stress Management - contrast between hypostress/'boreout' and hyperstress/ 'burnout' (unified by eustress/flow)
- Negotiation Strategy - contrast between win-lose and lose-win (unified by win-win scenarios)
- Problem-Solving - contrast between left-brain and right-brain (unified by whole-brain thinking)
- Skills Training - contrast between soft-skills/ 'high touch' and hard-skills/ 'high tech' (unified by high concept)

You get the drift.

Anyway, back to the Jedi. I came across a powerful passage in the Hagakure - that book most beloved of all real-life, wannabe Jedi - that speaks to this matter. I paraphrase it here:

"A monk cannot fulfill the Way if he does not manifest compassion

without and persistently store up courage within. And if a warrior does not manifest courage on the outside and hold enough compassion within his heart to burst his chest, he cannot become a samurai. Therefore, the monk pursues courage with the warrior as his model, and the warrior pursues the compassion of the monk."

A Jedi, then, is someone who seeks to live a life of *compassion* and *courage* - what we might today call empathy and resilience - in equal measure. Whether these two are brought together by balance or some other form of integration - such as perspectivism, as in "your focus determines your reality" - is something I don't yet know.

I'll be touching on some of this stuff - especially assertiveness and flow - in the forthcoming Jedi Knight Training Event in Belfast.

Chapter 54

The B Team

Allen's study.
Saturday 17 October 2009.

Despite more newspaper articles, quirky pictures, despite a new venue and an exciting syllabus, the swords, despite the fancy lightsabers and gadgets, despite the timing, the marketing, the potential, still it failed. A few phoned up to book, but not enough. So I'm feeling quite very pissed off.

Time to revert to plan B. Instead of one mega-event, a bi-weekly meeting of enthusiasts. Cheaper (for me and them). Easier to organize, no meals, no toys. Just like going to a Judo class only for Jedi. A mind-trick a week with role-playing and missions. I'll spread the word locally with Twitter and mail shots. Will it work?

My instincts tell me maybe in New York. It could in Northern Ireland if Mark Hamill himself was leading the class. Or even David Prowse. Feck it, the dwarf who did R2D2 would pile them in. But not otherwise. Not with me or my PhD. But I'm a teacher, dammit, not an actor! If I don't draft in the lowbrow, hi-concept edutainment then who will, eh, who will? Just tell me that!

No, in this country we won't have our boundaries blurred. These's us and them. North and South. There's work and there's play. Weekdays and weekends. School and fun. Reality versus hope. Nightmares over daydreams.

I'm waffling now, distorting my own distinctions.

I'm a trainer son, and I haven't had any dinner, so unless you want to chew bubblegum or kick ass, let me be.

Chapter 55

The Place of Power

Blog by Allen on 18 November 2009.

The Men Who Stare At Goats

A few years ago I bought my brother a book for Christmas called *The Men Who Stare At Goats*. I wanted to read it but was too stingy to spend the money on myself. So I bought it, 'carefully perused it make sure it was ok' and passed it on. Now it's out as a film with George Clooney and Ewan McGregor. It's about the US Army - which has a history for this sort of thing - attempting to train psychic warriors skills in the arts of remote viewing and other psychic abilities.

For some suspicious reason the entry on Project Jedi has been removed from Wikipedia but there are plenty of other sources of information. The article that started it all off in the *Journal of Non-*

lethal Combat is called, The First Earth Battalion: Dare to Think the Unthinkable, Ideas and Ideals for Soldiers Everywhere. And there is still a 1st Earth Battalion website. You can easily find them both through Google. So it must be true.

It's interesting to me that the army characters in the movie (and book) describe themselves as Jedi Masters - yet another measure of *Star Wars'* reach. And there is the usual link between Jedi powers and weird, new age type claims. It's a pity that wannabe Jedi don't focus their attentions instead on those 'powers' that are within everyone's potential: mindful awareness, intrinsic motivation, deep relaxation, empathic listening, open influencing, and the rest. Add to these some skills of memory, movement and language, and you're left with a very powerful person. No ESP required.

As far as super-hero powers go, it's often been observed that although Superman possesses near godlike abilities, what he does is mostly limited to rescuing the handbags of old ladies. In terms of culture-shaping influence, I could name half a dozen mortal, modern men - Marx, Darwin, Nietzsche, Freud, Newton, Ford - who are more powerful than any being Marvel or DC envisaged. Yoda could move an object with his mind, but he didn't move the minds of millions about how they viewed an object. *That* is power.

So what I'm saying is - enjoy the film as mindless fun, but if you want real power in life, don't stare at goats. Develop yourself instead. And if you want serious power, don't neglect the power of ideas, for they are the greatest Force in this universe of men.

Chapter 56

C = π D

Meeting Room, Blick Shared Studios, Belfast
Allen sits alone, waiting.

I'm parked here and I don't know if anyone is coming or not. That's the trouble with organizing an event like this with no enrollment or tickets. I could end up sitting at Blick Studios myself and looking like a complete norman no-mates.

Starting time was 7:30pm, twenty minutes ago.

It was always a half-baked idea. A dream. Better in my head than in reality. Who wants to train as a Jedi? Everyone. Until their time comes. Until it requires you to plan ahead and have your evening meal a little earlier or later than usual. Until you have to pay a price.

Wait, somebody walking through the door.

Me: "Hello."

Somebody: "Hello."

Me: "You here for the Jedi class?"

Somebody: "Yes."

Me: "Oh good, I didn't think anyone would turn up. By the looks of it, you're the first and the last."

Somebody: "How messianic of me."

Me: "Yea. I thought I recognised you."

Mark: "You do?"

Me: "You were at my Jedi workshop, the one at Queen's. You sat at the front and asked a lot of tricky questions."

Mark: "Did you mind?"

Me: "No, the opposite. Questions are good."

Mark: "Then here's one. Why was your last Jedi event a flop?"

Me: "Oh, straight in there. All right. Don't know for sure. Too expensive. No wow factor, no celebrity razzmatazz, no big names. Perhaps too cerebral despite the martial arts and samurai sword elements. People want actors signing autographs and storm-troopers running around to photograph and plastic light-saber duels at sunset."

Mark: "Maybe so but those aren't not the reasons you're looking for."

Me: "Enlighten me."

Mark: "You don't take it seriously enough."

Me: "Seriously enough? Look man, if I take it any more seriously, I'll be joining those brothers in Wales who think it's a religion. I think I've taken it way too seriously already. All the time and energy I've invested in this hasn't, you know, paid dividends."

Mark: "So it's all about, you know, dividends."

Me: "No. I wanted to make personal development fun, to link it with something people already recognised and were into. As clichéd as it sounds, I wanted to set imaginations on fire for learning. And who doesn't want to be a Jedi?"

Mark: "The entire population of Northern Ireland apparently. Except me."

Me: "So why did you turn up then?"

Mark: "Do you remember when we first made contact?"

Me: "Yea, at the Jedi course. You want to take a seat?"

Mark: "No, before then."

Me: "When?"

Mark: "I was signed up for a course you taught on power-plays. I wasn't able to get and asked you to send me on the notes. You obliged."

Me: "Oh. I don't remember."

Mark: "Reading your notes was a very powerful experience. They got me through a difficult time in my life."

Me: "Ah, I recall you saying something like that at the course. I couldn't work out if you were serious or not."

Mark rolls up his sleeves and reveals the scars.

"See that. That's as serious as it gets."

My eyes widen as I try to stare and look away at the same time. This is not an easy feat. "What happened?"

Mark: "Initiation. As one of your blogs calls it."

Me: "Initiation. Into what?"

Mark: "How seriously do you take it?"

Me: "What are you on about...?"

Mark: "How seriously?"

Me: "Not *that* seriously." (Indicating the scars.)

Mark: "That's why I'm stronger."

Me: "Dude, what is going on…"

Mark: "No. Not dude. Darth."

Me: "What?!?"

Mark: "Darth Obsidian."

Me: "Look, you need some sort of help."

Darth Obsidian: "I thought you preached the gospel of self-help, self-reliance. *I am it.*"

Long pause.

Me: "Right, could we just sit down and chat about this over coffee?"

Darth Obsidian: "No. There's been enough talk, enough teaching. Now is action time, the time for struggle and strife and creation. What is your name?"

Me: "You know its Allen…"

Darth Obsidian: "Your Jedi name."

Me: "My *Jedi* name? I don't have a *Jedi* name. There is no *Jedi!* They are not *real*."

Darth Obsidian: "I am Sith and I am real. How can there be Sith without Jedi, dark without light?"

Me: "It's only a fucking *film*, man!"

Darth Obsidian: "Young fool. After all you've taught. After all you've written. You still don't understand. If it's only a film, then answer me these questions, teacher. When you watch certain clips from the films, do you brim over with an irresistible wish in your heart *that these things were so?"*

Me: "Yes."

Darth Obsidian: "And is it so much a part of your mind that

you *dream* about it at night?"

Me: "Yes. But dreams are just made-up, make-believe."

Darth Obsidian: "Isn't it said that a goal is a dream with a deadline? My goal was to be the first Sith and I've already achieved it through steel and blood. Which makes you the first Jedi, if you chose to follow your destiny."

Me: "It's only a film."

Darth Obsidian: "I'm on the lookout for my first apprentice. I suggest you do the same. If you can find any."

Me: "It's only a film."

Darth Obsidian: "And get yourself a proper, Jedi name. 'Allen' makes you sound like a dentist."

Me: "Look, you're way out of…"

Darth Obsidian: "No, *you're* Luke. I'm offering you the chance to play hero here. What's stopping you?"

Me: "I don't want to…"

Darth Obsidian: "Don't lie to me, I can tell. And don't lie to yourself. You covet it. Tell me you don't crave to be Jedi and I shall quit. Say the words."

Me: "I…"

Darth Obsidian: "Say the words."

Long pause.

Me: "If I was a Jedi, my name would be Sadak Dorn."

Darth Obsidian: "So be it, Jedi."

Master Dorn: "What's next?"

Darth Obsidian: "I go to venerate Darth de Sales."

Master Dorn: "I don't know what that means, you literal bonehead!"

Darth Obsidian: "No. It is you that is ignorant. About a

great many things. Or so it is written."

And like that, poof, he's gone.

I sit around for a while after that, partly because I've paid my money for two hours and I want to use it up. But mostly to try and process what just transpired.

At around nine o'clock I develop the semblance of a smile on my lower lip due to a belief that I've cracked the code in his concluding quip and for other reasons I can't fully plumb and I walk out with a different point of view. And a new name. Not to mention a nemesis. OK for £20 expenditure and a vaguely sore head.

It's not every day you get to found an order of warrior-monks who serve as guardians of peace and justice throughout the galaxy.

It has to start somewhere, at some point in time, by some individual. Why not now? Why not me?

But not only me.

I need apprentices, lots of apprentices.

I need a way to bring them to me, a call to adventure.

I need to get the word out, to explain the whole tale from its beginning until now.

And I need a way to not look like a complete and utter knob-head with cocks on while doing all of the above.

By the time I drive home, a chronic case of the skeptics has set in, and I've given up on the whole idea as a shower of purest shite. I determine that if I ever meet that psycho again I'll do my darndest to introduce my foot to his face.

What a fantastic waste of my time, energy and reputation.

End of.

But still they linger.

What if? Why not? Who then? How to?

How to.

Chapter 57

What Is Thy Whill?

Upon reflection, my meeting with the other Force-wielder has left me, what? Exhilarated. Alive.

My meaning has been revealed to those who can read.

Which is what, my reader?

It is taught by those who know of such matters that the secrets of the Force were recorded in *The Journal of the Whilis*. It is the habit of many sentient beings to write, to tell their story in symbols and stories, in book format, even when there are other modes of documentation readily available.

I judge it a noble tradition and one worth following.

End Notes

Chapter 1: Vader on the Rocks

Men From Mars: How to Survive in a Strange World –

http://www.sensei-winbeforehand.co.uk/gender/men-from-mars/

Power-plays: How to Take Control in Life –

http://www.sensei-winbeforehand.co.uk/communication/how-to-take-control-in-life

Hyper-choice: Decision-making in a World f Alternatives –

http://www.sensei-winbeforehand.co.uk/news-and-events/hyper-choice/

I Think Therefore I Am: Brain Skills for Doers –

http://www.sensei-winbeforehand.co.uk/learning/i-think-therefore-i-am/

Chapter 2: All Men Dream

The Power of Humour: How to be Funny –

http://www.sensei-winbeforehand.co.uk/communication/funny-peculiar-or-funny-ha-ha

What Men Want: How to Manage the Men in Your Life –

http://www.sensei-winbeforehand.co.uk/gender/managemen

Body To Body: How to Communicate Without Words –

http://www.sensei-winbeforehand.co.uk/communication/body-language/body-to-body-funk-to-funky

Chapter 7: Master of My Universe

By the Power of Greyskull! –

http://www.sensei-winbeforehand.co.uk/news-and-events/power/

Confident Conversations: How to Talk in Any Situation –

http://www.sensei-

winbeforehand.co.uk/communication/confidentconversations/

Chapter 9: Angry Youngish Man

Men From Mars Waste Their Hours –

http://www.sensei-winbeforehand.co.uk/learning/men-from-mars-waste-

their-hours/

Why Are Men Such Fat, Stupid Wasters? #1 –

http://www.sensei-winbeforehand.co.uk/gender/why-are-men-such-fat-

stupid-wasters/

Why Are Men Such Fat, Stupid Wasters? #2 –

http://www.sensei-winbeforehand.co.uk/gender/why-are-men-such-fat-

stupid-wasters-2/

Chapter 10: Knowledge and Defence

The Psychology of Happiness: How to Grow Your Happy Skills

http://www.sensei-winbeforehand.co.uk/news-and-events/a-positive_y-

brilliant-workshop/

All Hail the Comedians!

http://www.sensei-winbeforehand.co.uk/communication/all-hail-the-

comedians/

The Main Thing: How to Find Meaning in Your Life

http://www.sensei-winbeforehand.co.uk/personal-development/the-making-of-meaning/

Chapter 13: Train Them You Can

Feel the Force: How to Train in the Jedi Way –
http://www.sensei-winbeforehand.co.uk/news-and-events/feel-the-force-how-to-train-in-the-jedi-way/

Students to learn the *Star Wars* way –
http://www.newsletter.co.uk/news/headlines/students-to-learn-the-star-wars-way-1-1874833

Yoda classes – how to be a Jedi –
http://news.bbc.co.uk/1/hi/northern_ireland/7597608.stm

Chapter 15: Stand Back Clive Owen!

Jedi Workshop Goes International! –
http://www.sensei-winbeforehand.co.uk/news-and-events/jedi-workshop-goes-international/

Will Jedi mind tricks attract male students? –
http://www.guardian.co.uk/education/2008/sep/09/3

The course with the Force: training Jedi style –
http://www.timeshighereducation.co.uk/story.asp?sectioncode=26&storycode=403508

University offers course in training the Jedi way –
http://www.thetimes.co.uk/tto/education/article1878456.ece

Star Wars Jedi Knights course offered by Queen's University Belfast –

http://www.telegraph.co.uk/education/2798657/Star-Wars-Jedi-Knights-course-offered-by-Queens-University-Belfast.html

Chapter 17: Serious Sci-Fi

Mind-tricks, Magic and the Media –
http://www.sensei-winbeforehand.co.uk/learning/mind-tricks-magic-and-the-media/

Bring your own light sabre: Uni launches Jedi course –
http://www.abc.net.au/news/2008-09-12/bring-your-own-light-sabre-uni-launches-jedi-course/507944

Magic 'boosts pupils' confidence' –
http://news.bbc.co.uk/1/hi/education/7612210.stm

Soon, kids to be trained the Jedi way for their personal development! –
http://www.thaindian.com/newsportal/india-news/soon-kids-to-be-trained-the-jedi-way-for-their-personal-development_10095172.html

UK Offering "How to Be a Jedi" College Course This Fall –
http://www.collegeotr.com/michigan_state_university/uk_offering_how_to_be_a_jedi_college_course_this_fall_11591

University Offers Jedi Training Course –
http://www.shortnews.com/start.cfm?id=73326

University offers one-day Jedi course –
http://www.theregister.co.uk/2008/09/12/jedi_course/

Star Wars Jedi Knights course offered by Queen's University –
http://www.reddit.com/r/WTF/comments/70ww1/star_wars_jedi_knights_course_offered_by_queens/%28comments%29

Become a Jedi Knight in One Easy Lesson –
http://io9.com/5048816/become-a-jedi-knight-in-one-easy-lesson

Queen's University Belfast Offers Jedi Knights Course –
http://www.jedinews.co.uk/news/news.aspx?newsID=1699

Chapter 19: The Sick Squid You Owe Me
Of Jedi Celebrities and *Star Wars* Actors –
http://www.sensei-winbeforehand.co.uk/news-and-events/of-jedi-
celebrities-and-star-wars-actors/

Chapter 20: A Cosm(et)ic Encounter
A Weekend With the Stars –
http://www.sensei-winbeforehand.co.uk/news-and-events/a-weekend-with-
the-stars/

Chapter 24: A Gaping Void
I'm Ok, You're an Introvert –
http://www.sensei-winbeforehand.co.uk/personal-
development/confidence/im-ok-youre-an-introvert/

The Most Pwerful Prefix in the Unvierse! –
http://www.sensei-winbeforehand.co.uk/learning/the-most-powerful-
prefix-in-the-universe/

Chapter 25: Chicks Send Me High
The Sultan's of Happiness –
http://www.sensei-winbeforehand.co.uk/learning/the-sultans-of-happiness/

Authentic Happiness –
http://www.sensei-winbeforehand.co.uk/personal-development/authentic-
happiness/

Happy Birthday Wikipedia! –
http://www.sensei-winbeforehand.co.uk/social-media/happy-birthday-wikipedia/

Chapter 26: Majordomo Zero

Assertiveness and Workplace Confidence –
http://www.sensei-winbeforehand.co.uk/communication/assertiveness-and-workplace-confidence/

5 Assertiveness Techniques –
http://www.sensei-winbeforehand.co.uk/communication/5-assertiveness-techniques/

How to Make Others Trust You –
http://www.sensei-winbeforehand.co.uk/communication/how-to-make-others-trust-you/

Chapter 27: As He Faced the Sun

Workplace Excellent With Emotional Intelligence –
http://www.sensei-winbeforehand.co.uk/personal-development/emotional-intelligence/ei/

How To Be Brave: The Return –
http://www.sensei-winbeforehand.co.uk/communication/assertiveness/how-to-be-brave-the-return/

You Wouldn't Like Me When I'm Angry –
http://www.sensei-winbeforehand.co.uk/communication/assertiveness/you-wouldnt-like-me-when-im-angry/

Chapter 28: Kansas Wizardry

Superman and Friends – The Ultimate Collection –
http://www.sensei-winbeforehand.co.uk/ethics/superman-and-friends-the-ultimate-collection/

Chapter 29: Eat the Census Takers

Ellen Langer Interview on Mindfulness –
http://www.sensei-winbeforehand.co.uk/personal-development/positive-psychology/ellen-langer-interview-on-mindfulness/

Chapter 33: Beware of Your Dreams

The UK's First University Jedi Course –
http://www.sensei-winbeforehand.co.uk/business/the-uks-first-university-jedi-course/

Chapter 35: Octavio Ocampo

Jedi Knights – Myth and Reality –
http://www.sensei-winbeforehand.co.uk/news-and-events/jedi-knights-myth-and-reality/

How to be Brave –
http://www.sensei-winbeforehand.co.uk/communication/how-to-be-brave/

Chapter 39: He That Has Ears

Star Wars Goes To Work –
http://www.sensei-winbeforehand.co.uk/communication/assertiveness/star-wars-goes-to-work/

Chapter 41: Cannot be Serious

Force is strong for Jedi police –
http://news.bbc.co.uk/1/hi/scotland/glasgow_and_west/8003067.stm

The Making of Meaning –
http://www.sensei-winbeforehand.co.uk/personal-development/the-making-of-meaning/

Chapter 43: You Will Be Assimilated
Storytelling, Innovation and Business –
http://www.sensei-winbeforehand.co.uk/news-and-events/storytelling-business-and-innovation/

Rory's Story Cubes –
http://www.storycubes.com/our-story/

Chapter 45: The Nanotech Ninja
Streetwise: How to Protect Yourself Against Aggression –
http://www.sensei-winbeforehand.co.uk/communication/assertiveness/streetwise-how-to-protect-yourself-against-aggression/

Sex and Self-Defence –
http://www.sensei-winbeforehand.co.uk/communication/assertiveness/sex-and-self-defence/

Belfast Aikido Circle –
http://bac.aikidoinireland.org/index.html

Colin Turner –
http://www.piglets.org/serendipity/pages/colin.html
http://www.piglets.org/serendipity/pages/colin.html

Chapter 46: Shadows and Dust
Mind Tricks and Mind Games

http://www.sensei-winbeforehand.co.uk/communication/assertiveness/mind-tricks-and-mind-games/

Chapter 47: Love Me Two Times
Jedi Knight Training in Belfast!
http://www.sensei-winbeforehand.co.uk/news-and-events/jedi-knight-training-event-in-belfast/

Chapter 51: Hoffer Meets Hannibal
To NLP or Not To NLP –
http://www.sensei-winbeforehand.co.uk/personal-development/to-nlp-or-not-to-nlp/

Chapter 53: Into Great Silence
The Way of the Warrior Monk –
http://www.sensei-winbeforehand.co.uk/personal-development/the-way-of-the-warrior-monk/

Chapter 55: The Place of Power
The Men Who Stare At Goats
http://www.sensei-winbeforehand.co.uk/personal-development/the-men-who-stare-at-goats/

Chapter 56: C = π D
Training As Initiation #1 –
http://www.sensei-winbeforehand.co.uk/learning/training-as-initiation-part-1/

3883054R00150

Printed in Great Britain
by Amazon.co.uk, Ltd.,
Marston Gate.